A SERIOUS CYCLIST'S GUIDE
to
SAN FRANCISCO and BEYOND

by

Jonathan Van Coops

REGENT PRESS
Berkeley, California

Copyright © 2024 by Jonathan Van Coops
ISBN 10: 1-58790-687-2
ISBN 13: 978-1-58790-687-9

Library of Congress Cataloging-in-Publication Data

Names: Van Coops, Jonathan, 1954- author.
Title: A serious cyclist's guide to San Francisco and beyond / by Jonathan Van Coops.
Description: Berkeley, California : Regent Press, [2024] | Includes index. | Summary: "Some of the most beautiful and challenging 'world-class' rides for any serious cyclist are found in the San Francisco Bay Area of California, USA. A Serious Cyclist's Guide to San Francisco and Beyond is intended for cyclists everywhere and presents maps, profiles photographs and detailed descriptions for sixteen memorable road bike rides in the San Francisco region, with routes covering about 900 miles and including over 59,000 feet of climbing. Geographically, the courses are situated within San Francisco, along the Marin and San Mateo County coasts and through the suburbs and parklands east of Berkeley, Oakland and San Jose. This set of rides presents a Central and South Bay complement to the many familiar North Bay 'wine country' rides found in Napa County and Sonoma County"-- Provided by publisher.
Identifiers: LCCN 2024031272 | ISBN 9781587906879 (trade paperback)
Subjects: LCSH: Cycling--California--San Francisco Bay Area--Guidebooks. | San Francisco Bay Area (Calif.)--Guidebooks.
Classification: LCC GV1045.5.C22 C2542 2024 | DDC 796.6409794/61--dc23/eng/20240703
LC record available at https://lccn.loc.gov/2024031272

All rights reserved.
No part of this book may be used or reproduced in any manner whatsoever without written permission except in the case of brief quotations embodied in articles and reviews. For information, write to Jonathan Van Coops at jonvc321@gmail.com.

Photographs by Thomas H. Mikkelsen and Frank Varvaro are used by permission of the photographers, who retain sole copyright to them. ©2024
Sole copyright to images by the author is retained by Jonathan Van Coops. ©2024

Printed and bound in the United States of America
Regent Press
Berkeley, California
www.regentpress.net
email: regentpress@mindspring.com

Contents

Introduction
Using this Guide   1
Essential Information   3
Map Legend   7
Map and Profile Notes   7

Rides: San Francisco and San Mateo Counties

1. Fort Point   9
2. Ocean Beach/Golden Gate Park   13
3. Lake Merced/Golden Gate Park   19
4. San Bruno Mountain   25
5. Skyline/Half Moon Bay   31
Crossing the Golden Gate Bridge   40

Rides: Marin County

6. Marin Headlands/Rodeo Lagoon   45
7. Tiburon Peninsula   51
8. Mount Tamalpais   57
9. Stinson Beach/Muir Beach   63
10. Point Reyes National Seashore   71
11. Marin French Cheese Company   79

Rides: Alameda, Contra Costa and Santa Clara Counties

12. The Three Bears/Briones Valley   89
13. Grizzly Peak/Reliez Valley   95
14. Mount Diablo   101
15. Morgan Territory Preserve   109
16. Mount Hamilton   115

Index of Selected Places	119
Appendix 1: List of Bike Shops	121
About the Author	123
Acknowledgements	124

List of Ride Maps

Ride Locator Map

1.	Fort Point	8
2.	Ocean Beach/Golden Gate Park	12
3.	Lake Merced/Golden Gate Park	18
4.	San Bruno Mountain	24
5.	Skyline/Half Moon Bay	30

Golden Gate Bridge Map — 42

6.	Marin Headlands/Rodeo Lagoon	44
7.	Tiburon Peninsula	50
8.	Mount Tamalpais	56
9.	Stinson Beach/Muir Beach	62
10.	Point Reyes National Seashore	70
11.	Marin French Cheese Company	78
12.	The Three Bears/Briones Valley	88
13.	Grizzly Peak/Reliez Valley	94
14.	Mount Diablo	100
15.	Morgan Territory Preserve	108
16.	Mount Hamilton	

Introduction

I am a life-long serious cyclist, a medium to long-distance road bicyclist. I grew up riding the city streets in San Francisco's East Bay area beginning in 1963. I learned to ride in a day and have never stopped pedaling through the years. I'm also a fourth-generation local boy — a descendent of families that came to San Francisco in the mid-19th and early 20th centuries. I live here — I ride here — I've ridden all of the rides included in this guide. My bikes and I have traversed the City and its hinterlands for decades.

I began riding routinely into the hilly Regional Park lands east of Berkeley about 1970. A decade later I moved across the bay to Marin, where I rode hundreds of miles a year throughout the County and the Napa/Sonoma wine country. After relocating to San Francisco in the 90s, I added the Peninsula and San Mateo coast to my repertoire of routine jaunts. I still love riding in the City — along the Bay to the Golden Gate and through the Presidio to Golden Gate Park.

In addition to being a local and a lover of cycling, I am a professional cartographer — a map maker and geographer — who had a lengthy career involved in all aspects of mapping California's Coastal Zone.[1] Through my employment, I became even more familiar with the geography of the San Francisco Bay area. It was my good fortune to be the principal cartographer for many successful coastal map and guidebooks between 1980 and 2015, when I retired.

Since then, having not only time to ride but to write, I decided to use my technical abilities and geographic expertise to produce a unique cycling guide book for the part of the San Francisco Bay region that I know best. Of course, there are many other great rides and cycling guides available, particularly for the North Bay wine country, so my goal was to describe a number of other fantastic regional rides. I became convinced that, with effective maps, photos and informative ride descriptions, I could create a memoir of my own favorite rides in the form of a useful guide book — of value to any serious cyclist interested in the San Francisco area's exceptional bicycling opportunities.

A Serious Cyclist's Guide to San Francisco and Beyond is intended to showcase sixteen of the region's remarkable 'world-class' rides. My hope is that I've presented them in a manner that contributes to a better understanding and appreciation of the premium cycling possible here in the Bay Area — rides that convey the visual beauty of the region, provide grand vistas, exhilarating descents and also require a mixture of good equipment, honed riding skills, fitness and commitment.

Jonathan Van Coops
San Francisco, March 2024

---

[1] The California Coastal Zone extends over 1100 miles along the State's shore and includes over 1.3 million acres (526,000 hectares) of adjacent inland areas within the fifteen coastal and nine San Francisco Bay Area counties.

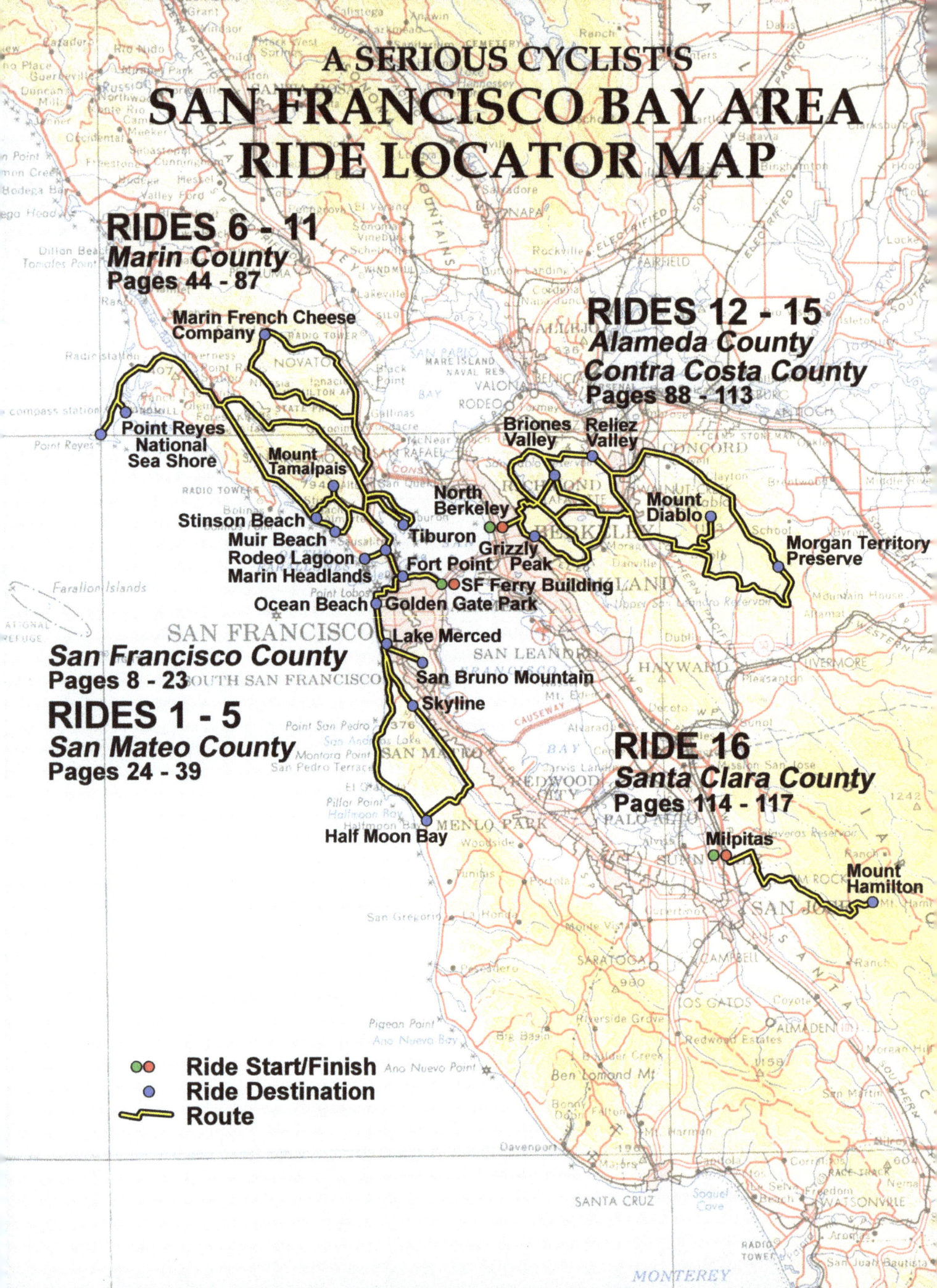

Using the Guide

A Serious Cyclist's Guide to San Francisco and Beyond is a tool for planning extraordinary and challenging cycling experiences in the central and south San Francisco Bay region. The frontispiece is a ride locator map depicting the sixteen routes. The rides are located in San Francisco, San Mateo, Marin, Alameda, Contra Costa and Santa Clara Counties.

The Ride Summary on the following page depicts all of the rides at the same scale and shows three shorter, flatter rides in and around San Francisco, a medium-distance hill climb, a longer day-ride south on the San Mateo Coast, six medium and longer-distance bay and coastal rides in Marin County, four hilly, medium and long-distance rides in Alameda and Contra Costa Counties and a single medium-distance ride in Santa Clara County — climbing to the highest elevation in the Bay Area. The total distance for all sixteen rides is about 900 miles. Total climbing is over 59,000 feet.

The windy, hilly 120-mile ride to Point Reyes in west Marin County is perhaps the most challenging, though some may consider the ride to the summit of Mount Diablo, with over 7000 feet of climbing, to be the most difficult. Then there is Mount Hamilton! However, distance and climbing are only two aspects of a ride. Each of the rides follows a route where weather, terrain, and traffic — together with one's level of fitness and determination — combine to reward a cyclist willing to explore a variety of distances, challenging climbs and exhilarating descents. The result is ultimately a sense of accomplishment, especially true for the rides requiring more physical ability and preparation.

The San Francisco, San Mateo and Marin rides are staged from the Ferry Building in San Francisco, near Justin Herman Plaza and the foot of Market Street. The East Bay rides begin and end at the+ North Berkeley BART Station. All of the start/finish points are accessible via BART[2] and most rides may be adapted to begin or end at nearby BART stations located in downtown San Francisco (Embarcadero and Daly City stations) and the East Bay (El Cerrito, North Berkeley, Orinda, Lafayette, Pleasant Hill stations). The South Bay ride to Mount Hamilton is staged from the Milpitas BART station.

Each ride is mapped and described in detail. Map scales vary according to ride distance. Profiles indicate elevations along the route. Ride descriptions include:

1. Outstanding ride characteristics and challenges: distance, climbing, views, wind and weather. Selected points of interest en route.
2. Detailed Route Directions: start/finish, turning points and destinations.
3. Road Character: road surface, riding space; terrain and physical geography (flat, rolling, steady uphill, steep mountain section, sustained difficult climb, etc.).
4. Climbing: total elevation gain, in feet.[3]
5. Riding situation (i.e., traffic, pedestrians, etc.) and specific road conditions (i.e., gradient, technical, light/shade, narrow, rough, hazards, wet/slippery).
6. Unique or notable ride information regarding – approximate ride times, rest stops and available services.

---

[2] Bay Area Rapid Transit.
[3] 3.281 feet equals one meter.

1

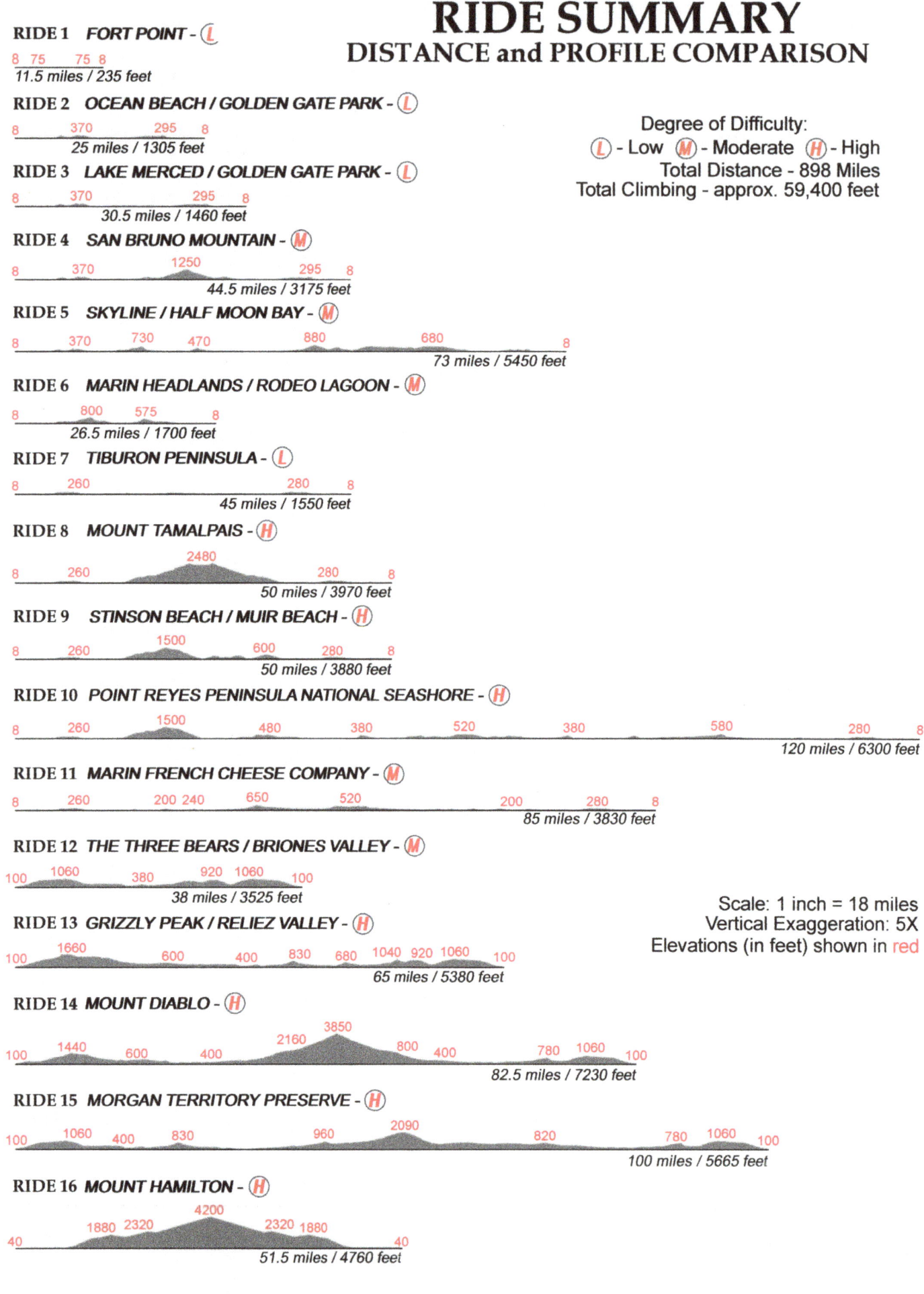

Essential Information

The San Francisco Bay Area provides great cycling opportunities for riders of all levels. The serious cyclist can find truly remarkable rides in the central and south bay counties. Each of the sixteen rides included in the guide can provide memorable, unique experiences. Some help develop increased fitness and endurance — others *require* it. Any of the rides can be made part of a training regimen or considered as individual accomplishments.

No matter how serious a cyclist may be, tourists, racers and casual riders will all experience cycling through the City, urban suburbs and rural areas of the San Francisco region as something that does *not* discriminate. Cycling in the Bay Area can be quite complicated for anyone and just as challenging for one type of rider as another. Weather, terrain, time of day and year, traffic, one's level of fitness, determination and preparation each vary but combine to affect every ride. Even bike *services* vary from place to place.[4]

Road Conditions

Well-paved streets, bike lanes and paths can be the norm in parts of the San Francisco Bay Area but the opposite is just as common in many communities. Debris, broken asphalt, patches and potholes of many sizes can be found throughout the network of streets and roads in the region. Less-frequently maintained segments of narrow and winding road are also found in *all* of the urban and rural rides included in this guide. Steep, hairpin, switchback turns can be 'off-camber' on older mountain roads, making descents tricky and technical. California's vehicle code allows bicyclists 'full use of a traffic lane,' however, similar to riding 'legally' on a highway shoulder, it's really best to do this only when safe and/or necessary.

Weather Conditions

The San Francisco region's climate is classified as *inland* or *coastal* Mediterranean, depending on location. With its 'inverted' precipitation regime, a seasonal drought is typical in the summer months, which can be hot and dry inland, while cool and fog-shrouded on the coast. Prevailing winds are often westerly but vary depending on time of day and year, weather conditions and elevation. Most rain comes during Winter and Spring but slick, wet road conditions are common all year in wooded and fog-prone areas.

The Mediterranean climates are rare, occurring in only a handful of areas around the world outside of the region of the Mediterranean Sea, itself. They are also considered one of the most variable climates on the planet, meaning that the weather conditions are highly-changeable. To complicate things further, the mountain geography of the California's Coast Range and Diablo Range helps create a pattern of many microclimates that extends from west Marin and the San Mateo Coast throughout the region. Many consider Spring and Fall the best seasons for cycling in the Bay Area. Others believe 'there's never a *bad* time to ride.' Nevertheless, it's always a good idea to bring a vest and sunscreen. Afternoon sea breezes from the west can often produce chaotic headwinds.

---

[4] A partial list of San Francisco Bay Area bike shops located within some proximity to the ride routes is included as Appendix 1.

Riding Etiquette

Thanks to many forces operating the wheels of activism, bureaucracy and politics over time, construction of separated bike lanes, painting and signage and other improvements to the network of Bay Area bike paths, lanes, and trails are all taking place with increasing regularity. There are sometimes exceptions, however, usually riding in the bike lane — where parallel to a bike path or multi-use trail — is preferred for the routes described.
— Avoid riding on sidewalks. Reduce speed on bridges, bike paths and multi-use trails.
— Watch for children, pets, or parents making sudden, unexpected moves.
— Watch for pedestrians with strollers; be extra careful, the child may not be in it.
— Pass on the left. Slow or stop as far to the right as possible.

Rest Stops

Short breaks off the bike and at destinations present good opportunities to put on a jacket, stretch, drink or eat something. Ten to fifteen minutes is usually enough time to rest and check the bike quickly before beginning to ride again. Most of the rides reach destination points at roughly half of the full distance. Starting the return ride *before* your body cools off is recommended. Afternoon headwinds are common on many of the return routes.

Safety

Any serious cyclist is aware that riding conditions are by nature highly dynamic. One of the most enjoyable elements of cycling is the changing landscape and experiences one has while rolling along. Factors we don't control, such as the amount of traffic, weather and road conditions, greatly affect how safely one can ride but there are still things that cyclists can and should do, before *and* during riding, to help ensure an enjoyable ride and a safe return to the start point.

Safety off the bike and before the ride
— Check the bike mechanically; clean, lubricate, adjust derailleurs and brakes.
— Check tires and wheels. Wheels should be true, spokes tensioned; Tires should have adequate tread and proper air pressure.
— Any mounted equipment should be checked and secured if necessary (racks, lights, water bottles, handlebar-mounted equipment, helmet camera).
— If needed, check your ride's route map; Plan stop locations and locate bike shops.
— Prepare a tool kit that includes two (2) tubes, a patch kit, CO_2 cartridges (optional), tire levers, hex or Allen wrenches, a chain link tool, two (2) extra links of chain, spoke wrench, a pump and any other necessary tools (screwdrivers, wrenches).
— Pack adequate food and drink for the ride length and difficulty.
— Check the weather forecast and be prepared for changing conditions; Pack arm warmers, leg warmers, windbreaker, rain jacket and sunscreen, as needed.
— Maximize visibility for drivers by wearing bright clothing and bike gear reflectors. Use lights for any low-visibility riding, especially at dusk or later in the evening.
— A bell, small, but loud enough to be heard by drivers, pedestrians, children, pets, and other cyclists is often a useful item when riding in congested areas or multi-use trails.

Safety on the bike and while riding
— Wear a helmet.
— Be prepared to perform some roadside repairs. Check tires and wheels at rest stops.
— Carry Identification, health insurance and emergency contact information, phone, money, keys.
— Stay alert and focused on surroundings; don't use earbuds or earphones while cycling.
— Be aware of aggressive and unaware drivers.
— In the United States, like many countries, where streets and roads meet, motor vehicle traffic approaching from the right has priority to continue or proceed first if stopped at the intersection. Yield the right of way to traffic coming from this direction.
— Use maneuvers that keep you visible to drivers – don't follow too close, avoid riding in blind spots and, if possible, follow so that you remain visible in a vehicle's side and rear view mirrors, especially while descending.
— Ride single file when riding in groups.

Vehicles turning Right at a Red-light Signal in California
Unless signed and specifically prohibited, California law allows for motor vehicles to turn right, after stopping, at a red light signal. It's often prudent for cyclists to stop or wait for a green light signal at a distance *before* the intersection, avoiding the risk of being cut off or possibly injured by cars entering the bike lane in order to turn right.

Even when riding within a bike lane, cars to your left moving in the same direction may enter the lane, cross in front of you, and turn right into a driveway or intersecting street. They may signal and look over their shoulder before turning but, especially in thick traffic, it's always a good idea to expect that unaware drivers may slow and begin turning *before* they signal or look.

Make a habit of visually checking the front wheels of vehicles moving ahead slowly, close to or alongside the bike lane. This will reveal vehicle's steering movement and direction, regardless of turn signals and driver actions.

Avoiding 'The Door'
Always use caution when maneuvering around parked and double-parked vehicles, or other large vehicles (e.g., articulated buses and delivery trucks). As mentioned above, vehicle laws in California allow cyclists full use of the traffic lane and require drivers to enter and exit their vehicles in a safe manner, however, many a cyclist has been 'doored' while proceeding around and past a parked vehicle whose driver quickly opened the door without first looking to see if it was safe or whether a bike or other vehicle was approaching. Always watch for drivers sitting in parked cars and use caution when occupying the full traffic lane to pass stopped or parked vehicles.

Rush-hour Riding
Rush-hour riding or getting caught in any commute along streets with or without bike lanes is almost always hectic to harrowing — anything but fun. Unless absolutely impossible, adjust rides times to avoid the problems of rush-hour riding. Be prepared to use extreme caution in those circumstances where it is necessary. Traffic islands, steel grates and manhole covers can all become obstacles when vehicle traffic is thick.

A Safety Mindset

— Be alert and ready for drivers, pedestrians, and even other cyclists to make sudden, unexpected actions. Expect unintended circumstances!

— Remember the words of an old bike shop owner — 'It's the surprises that'll get you!'

— Be aware of the safety element that relates to the acts of others but pay attention to those elements we can have control over: equipment function, preparation and familiarity with ride/route conditions, fitness level and riding style.

— It's a bike! — and can be walked or carried, if necessary.

Security

The San Francisco Bay Area may or may *not* be considered a bicycle thieves' paradise by those who live or ride here. Nevertheless, at least two things are certain: (1) A lot of bikes *do* get stolen; and (2) The cost of bikes ridden by most cyclists has increased by at least a factor of *twenty* since the 1960s! All things considered, if a serious cyclist's bicycle gets stolen, it's likely to be an expensive and emotional loss.

Even if insured, it's never a good idea to leave a beloved bike unattended and unlocked — anywhere. *Attended* and unlocked — maybe briefly —, while it's attended by someone you know and trust, who keeps it in constant view. Well-locked and *unattended* – maybe — for a very short while (e.g., five minutes or less), preferably while in it remains in view.

It's really not worth the risk of losing a bike. If you ride a valuable bike — keep it safe when you're out, by *not* leaving it anywhere for too long, whether locked or not.

San Francisco Ferry Building / Embarcadero Plaza

North Berkeley BART Station

Milpitas BART Station

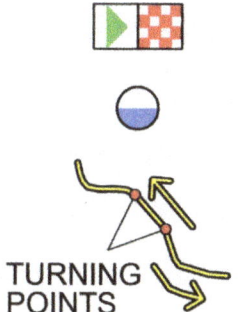

Map Notes
1. Ride maps are scaled to show entire rides with a minimum of overlap. A graphic scale indicates distance in statute miles.
2. Segments of ride routes have been ridden, walked or driven during 2022 and 2023. Map descriptions reflect conditions at that time. *Check route ahead of time for current street and road conditions.*
3. Base map images are from public domain sources.

Profile Notes
1. Profiles are based on elevations at locations along each of the sixteen ride routes. Elevations values are given in feet above mean sea level. Distances are shown in statute miles.
2. Profiles convey the general character of the terrain covered in each ride. Selected high and low elevation points are labeled.
3. In order to create visually useful ride profiles an appropriate ratio of elevation *and* distance must be chosen. All profiles require some degree of vertical exaggeration in order to effectively depict elevation changes.
4. A vertical exaggeration of approximately *10x* is used for *all* of the ride profiles. As a result, if *one horizontal inch* represents a chosen distance (e.g., one mile[5]), then *ten inches* would represent that same distance in the *vertical* dimension.

---

[5] One mile equals 5280 feet and 1.61 kilometers.

RIDE 1 : FORT POINT

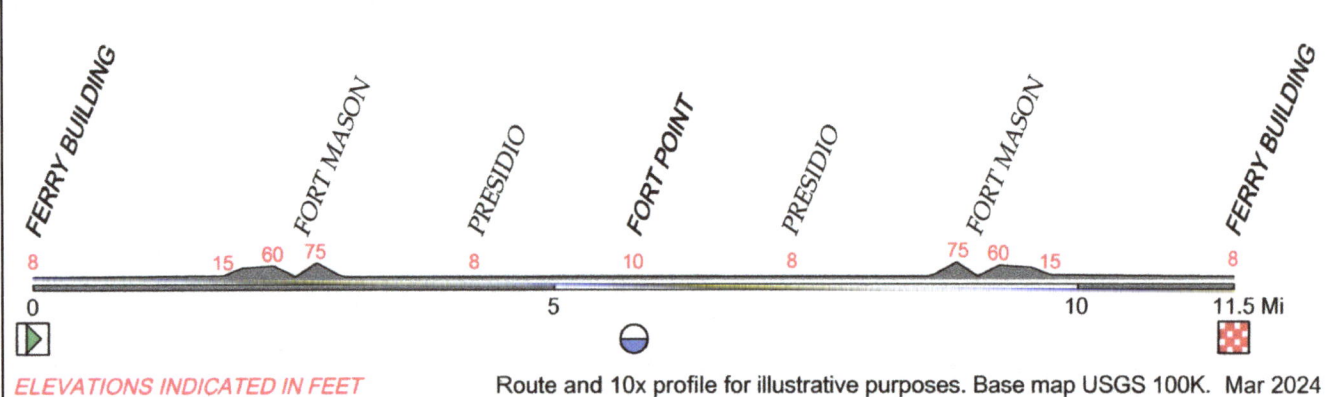

ELEVATIONS INDICATED IN FEET Route and 10x profile for illustrative purposes. Base map USGS 100K. Mar 2024

Ride 1: Fort Point

This waterfront ride follows a familiar route from the downtown San Francisco Ferry Building to the Fort Point National Historic Site, directly below the Golden Gate Bridge. When the weather cooperates, one can enjoy the scenic bay shoreline views found along this course — well-suited for a short, flat workout or simply a convenient way to spin the legs and get some fresh air. Cyclists at a basic fitness level can complete this 11.5 mile ride in less than two hours and while not particularly strenuous, urban riding, often windy conditions and several brief, steeper sections provide some challenges. This ride covers the beginning and ending segments for the other rides situated in San Francisco, San Mateo and Marin Counties.

The route begins at the San Francisco Ferry Building and proceeds north and west along the Bay, through Fort Mason and the Marina District into the Presidio of San Francisco, along the bay shoreline to the Fort Point National Historic Site. The return follows the same course in reverse: through the Presidio and Fort Mason, then along the City's northern waterfront to Justin Herman Plaza, at the foot of Market Street.

San Francisco Municipal Pier / Aquatic Park

Ride Characteristics

Difficulty: Low

Distance: 11.5 miles

Terrain: Mostly flat, with two gradual uphill sections and one short, steep uphill and descent within Fort Mason.

Elevation Range: Approximately 8 feet to 75 feet above sea level.

Climbing: Approx. 235 feet

Situation: Urban and urban parkland setting.

Road Conditions: Street traffic and pedestrians — moderate to heavy; road surfaces — good to rough, slippery on foggy or overcast wet morning descents through wooded parklands.

Weather: Sea breezes off the bay and ocean can provide a substantial wind factor. Fort Point can often be cool and foggy during the summer.

Notes: Bike shops numbered 1 through 7 in Appendix 1 are found in the general vicinity traversed along this route through San Francisco. Nevertheless, shops are not always open or nearby — carrying essential tools, a pump, a tire repair kit and 2 tubes is recommended.

Approximate Ride Time: 1 to 1.5 hours.

San Francisco Bay Trail / Upper Fort Mason

Detailed Route Directions

Begin the ride in front of the Ferry Building and proceed north along the Embarcadero using the two-way, signed and green-painted bike lane. This lane is preferable for most cyclists, compared to the heavily-walked San Francisco Bay Trail segment located along the east sidewalk of the Embarcadero. The bike lane becomes one-way 'northbound' at Broadway. Continue in the bike lane to North Point Street. Use the signed and painted bike lane to cross the Embarcadero and turn left on to North Point Street. Ride along North Point Street, climbing steadily for two blocks at Columbus Avenue and continuing past Ghirardelli Square to Van Ness Avenue. Turn right on Van Ness Avenue and descend two blocks to its end, at the Aquatic Park Municipal Pier.

Turn left before the pier and ride into Fort Mason. The short climb up the former McDowell Avenue and around Black Point requires about five minutes of riding in a low gear or pedaling out of the saddle to gain about 65 feet of elevation. Watch for pedestrians and other cyclists walking bikes or those who stop along the San Francisco Bay Trail to view the Golden Gate Bridge. Other bicyclists may also stop suddenly on the steep incline after neglecting to shift into an easier gear. Still other cyclists may be descending rapidly from the opposite direction.

On a clear day, cyclists will enjoy stunning vistas of San Francisco Bay and the Golden Gate Bridge before descending past Fort Mason's Great Meadow to the pan-flat Marina Boulevard. This part of the route is just eight to ten feet above the bay's elevation. Proceed along Marina Boulevard past Gaslight Cove, the Marina Green and the St. Francis Yacht Club into the Presidio, where Marina Boulevard intersects Old Mason Street at Yacht Road.

Follow Old Mason Street through the Presidio adjacent to the restored wetlands and Crissy Field, then along a segment of the San Francisco Bay Trail or through the West Bluff Picnic Area parking lot, past the National Park's popular 'Warming Hut' to Marine Drive. Watch for pedestrians and waves breaking over the seawall while continuing along Marine Drive to the Fort Point National Historic Site[6] — destination and turnaround point of the ride. Whether the skies are

---

[6] The masonry fortification was built by US Army Engineers between 1853 and 1861 and designated a National Historic Site in 1970.

foggy or clear, it's a great spot for photos of the nineteenth-century fort building, the bay shoreline and the Golden Gate Bridge.

The return route from the National Historic Site follows the previous directions in their reverse order. Ride along Marine Drive, then Old Mason Street, to Marina Boulevard. Continue east on Marina Boulevard to Fort Mason. Climb along the San Francisco Bay Trail through upper Fort Mason, past the Great Meadow and around Black Point, before descending to Van Ness Avenue to North Point Street. Turn left on North Point Street and continue to the Embarcadero. Turn right on the Embarcadero and proceed to finish the ride at Justin Herman Plaza, just west of the Ferry Building.

Fort Point National Historic Site / Marine Drive

Fort Point National Historic Site / Golden Gate Bridge

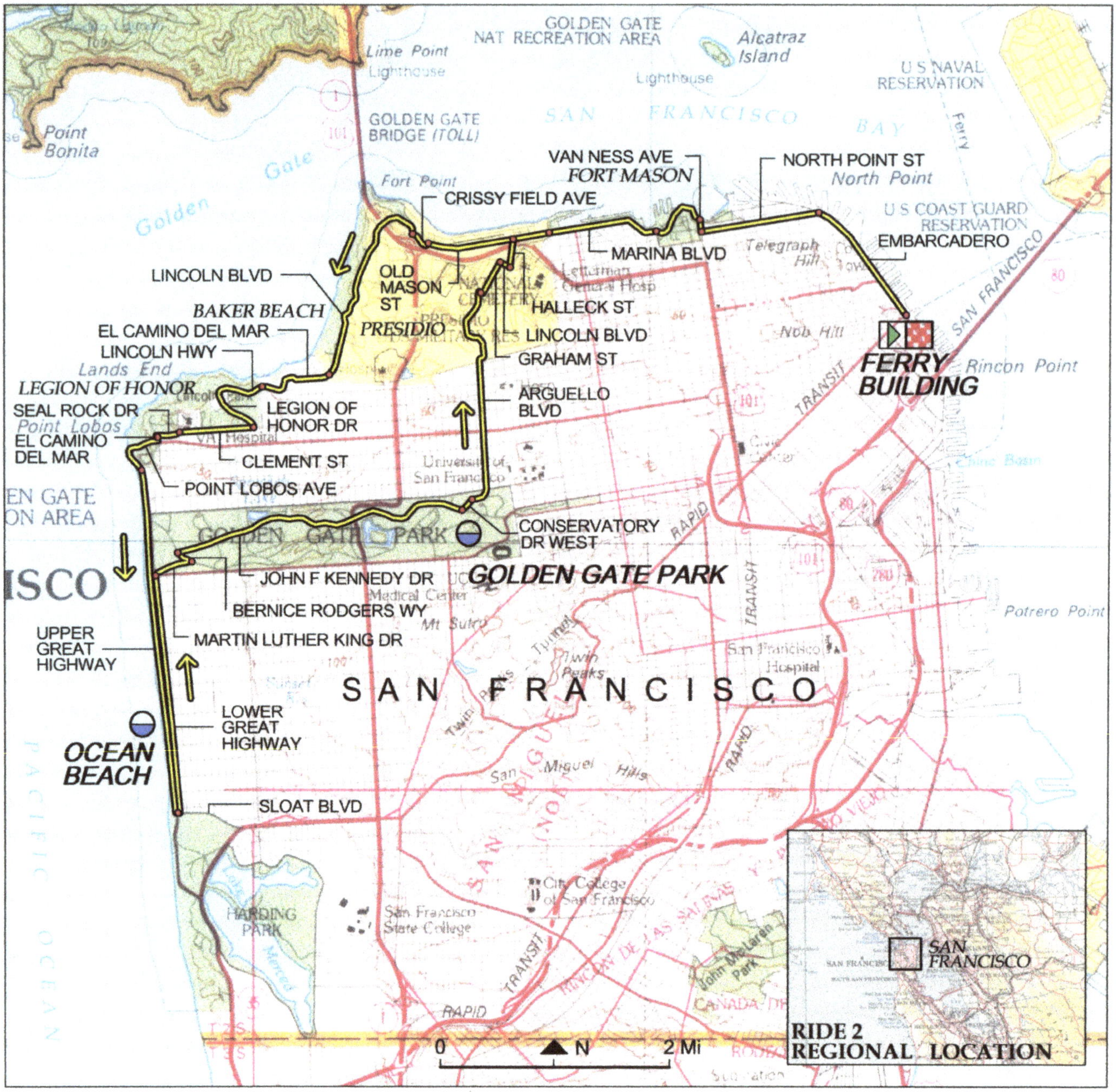

RIDE 2: OCEAN BEACH / GOLDEN GATE PARK

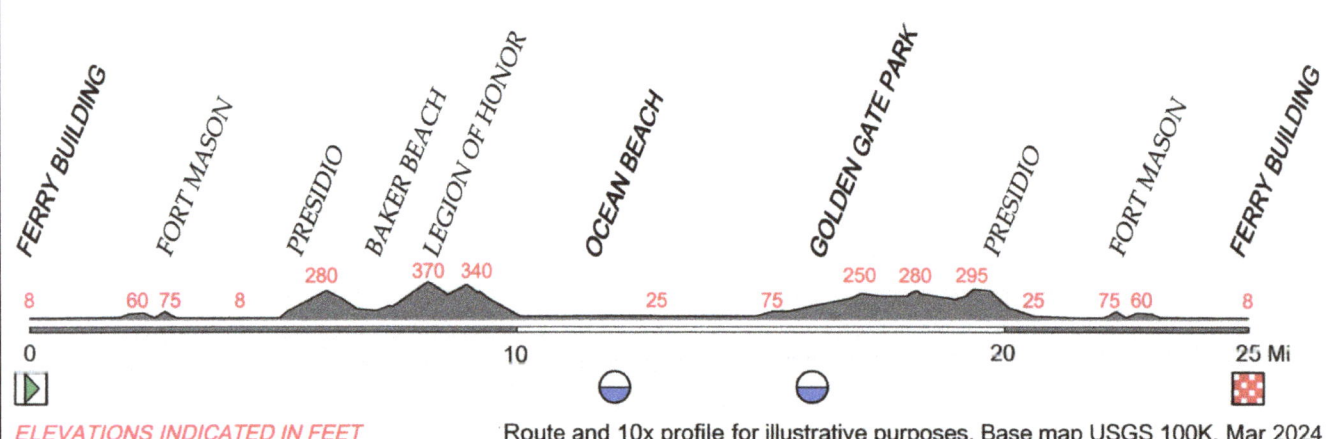

ELEVATIONS INDICATED IN FEET — Route and 10x profile for illustrative purposes. Base map USGS 100K. Mar 2024

Ride 2: Ocean Beach/Golden Gate Park

This ride is a familiar San Francisco jaunt for many cyclists, one well-suited as either a short, mostly flat training workout or a convenient route for a weekend ride and picnic in Golden Gate Park. Particularly when weather cooperates, everyone can enjoy the picturesque bay and coastal shoreline cycling found along this beautiful scenic route. Many riders at a moderate fitness level can do this 25 mile ride in less than two hours and while not the most demanding of rides, there are several brief but steep sections providing just over 1300 feet of climbing, potentially windy conditions, and enough urban and urban parkland riding to guarantee a sense of challenge. This ride also includes the core route segments for the other three rides situated in San Francisco and San Mateo Counties.

The route begins at the San Francisco Ferry Building and proceeds north and west along the Bay into the Presidio of San Francisco towards the Golden Gate Bridge — then through the Sea Cliff neighborhood and Lincoln Park, past the Palace of the Legion of Honor, the former Cliff House restaurant and along the Upper Great Highway past Ocean Beach to Sloat Boulevard. The return takes riders north on the Lower Great Highway, then through Golden Gate Park, the Presidio and along the City's northern waterfront to Justin Herman Plaza, at the foot of Market Street.

Greater Farallones Visitor Center, Crissy Field, the Presidio Shoreline and Downtown San Francisco

Ride Characteristics
Difficulty: Low
Distance: 25 miles
Terrain: Mostly flat, with several gradual uphill sections and short, steep climbing and descending sections within Fort Mason, the Presidio, and Golden Gate Park.
Elevation Range: Approximately 8 feet to 370 feet above sea level.

Climbing: Approx. 1305 feet

Situation: Urban and urban parkland setting.

Road Conditions: Street traffic and pedestrians — moderate to heavy; road surfaces — good to rough, slippery on foggy or overcast wet-morning descents through wooded parklands.

Weather: Sea breezes off the bay and ocean can provide a substantial wind factor. Morning conditions can often be cool and cloudy.

Notes: Bike shops numbered 1 through 16 in Appendix 1 are found in the general vicinity traversed along this route through San Francisco. Nevertheless, shops are not always open or nearby — carrying essential tools, a pump, a tire repair kit and 2 tubes is recommended.

Approximate Ride Time: 1.5 - 2 hours.

Detailed Route Directions

Begin the ride in front of the Ferry Building and proceed north along the Embarcadero using the two-way signed and green-painted bike lane. This lane is preferable for most cyclists, compared to the heavily-walked San Francisco Bay Trail segment located along the east sidewalk of the Embarcadero. The bike lane becomes one way 'northbound' at Broadway. Continue in the bike lane to North Point Street. Use the signed and painted bike lane to cross the Embarcadero and turn left on to North Point Street. Ride along North Point Street, climbing steadily for two blocks at Columbus Avenue and continuing past Ghirardelli Square to Van Ness Avenue. Turn right on Van Ness Avenue and descend two blocks to its end, at the Aquatic Park Municipal Pier.

Turn left before the pier and ride into Fort Mason. The short climb up the former McDowell Avenue and around Black Point requires about five minutes of riding in a low gear or pedaling out of the saddle to gain about 65 feet of elevation. Watch for pedestrians and other cyclists walking bikes or those who stop along the San Francisco Bay Trail to view the Golden Gate Bridge. Other bicyclists may also stop suddenly on the steep incline after neglecting to shift into an easier gear. Still other cyclists may be descending rapidly from the opposite direction.

On a clear day, cyclists will enjoy stunning vistas of San Francisco Bay and the Golden Gate Bridge before descending past Fort Mason's Great Meadow to the pan-flat Marina Boulevard. This part of the route is just eight to ten feet above the bay's elevation. Proceed along Marina Boulevard past Gaslight Cove, the Marina Green and the St. Francis Yacht Club into the Presidio, where Marina Boulevard intersects Old Mason Street at Yacht Road.

Follow Old Mason Street through the Presidio adjacent to the restored wetlands and Crissy Field, turn left and then quickly right on to Crissy Field Avenue and climb the short, steep pitch a few hundred feet to Lincoln Boulevard. Having gained about fifty feet of elevation, turn right at the stop sign and follow Lincoln Boulevard, climbing gradually past the Golden Gate Bridge and reaching an elevation of about 250 feet before descending through the western Presidio past Baker Beach. Climb gradually once again into the Sea Cliff neighborhood where Lincoln Boulevard intersects Camino del Mar at about 100 feet elevation. Continue through Sea Cliff along Camino del Mar into Lincoln Park.

Once in Lincoln Park, Camino del Mar becomes Lincoln Highway and climbs steadily to the Palace of the Legion of Honor at about 350 feet elevation — also the high point of the ride. South of the Legion of Honor, the road, now called Legion of Honor Drive, descends to the intersection of Thirty-Fourth Avenue and Clement Street. Exit Lincoln Park and turn right onto Clement Street. Continue on the mild but steady incline to approximately 300 feet elevation at Forty-Sixth Avenue where Clement Street becomes Seal Rock Drive. Continue on Seal Rock Drive and descend to Camino Del Mar. Turn left, continuing one block on Camino del Mar to Point Lobos Avenue. Turn right on to Point Lobos Avenue.

Point Lobos Avenue presents a fast descent past the very popular Golden Gate National Recreational Area (GGNRA) Visitor Center and the former Cliff House restaurant.

Ocean Beach and the Great Highway

Watch for pedestrians, slow moving tour buses, cabs, and people backing out of the diagonal parking spaces along the seaward side of the street while proceeding south to the Great Highway just inland of Ocean Beach.

The last section before beginning the return is a straight, flat three miles, along the upper Great Highway past Ocean Beach to Sloat Boulevard. With timed traffic signals and a decent tailwind, this section can be a great place to really get rolling, however, watch for fast-moving cars, rough pavement and sand blown on to the road, especially south of Golden Gate Park, where occasional road closures force traffic to use the landward and parallel *lower* Great Highway. For a quick rest stop, turn right into the GGNRA parking lot at Sloat Boulevard — destination point of the ride.

To return, cross the Great Highway and ride east one block on Sloat Boulevard to Forty-Seventh Avenue. After making a U-turn on Sloat Boulevard, proceed half a block and turn right on to the *lower* Great Highway. Ride along the lower Great Highway to Kirkham Street. At Kirkham Street, bear right on La Playa Street and continue north. Follow La Playa Street to Lincoln Way and cross into Golden Gate Park. Make a short, gradual climb past the Murphy Windmill along Martin Luther King Jr. Drive to Bernice Rodgers Way. Turn left and ride a few hundred meters past Spreckels Lake to John F. Kennedy Drive and turn right.

Continue through the park on John F. Kennedy Drive to the Conservatory of Flowers, turn left on Conservatory Drive West and climb the short rise to Arguello Boulevard. A short descent on Arguello Boulevard leads out of the park at Fulton Street.

Continue on Arguello Boulevard. North of Clement Street, Arguello Boulevard rises steadily, and then climbs abruptly for one steep block between Washington Street and Jack-

Spreckels Lake / Golden Gate Park

son Street, reaching an elevation of about 300 feet just south of the Presidio entrance. Once inside the Presidio, continue along a flat section of Arguello Boulevard, before descending rapidly to the Main Post at elevation 100 feet. Brake carefully and turn right on to Moraga Avenue at the bottom of Arguello Boulevard, then turn quickly left on Graham Street in front of the Presidio Officer's Club. Follow Graham Street to Lincoln Boulevard, turn right on Lincoln Boulevard and continue to Girard Road. Turn left on Girard Road which then becomes Marina Boulevard.

Continue east on Marina Boulevard to Fort Mason. Climb along the San Francisco Bay Trail through upper Fort Mason, past the Great Meadow and around Black Point, before descending to Van Ness Avenue and the foot of the Aquatic Park Municipal Pier. Climb gradually two blocks on Van Ness Avenue to North Point Street. Turn left and continue along North Point Street to the Embarcadero. Turn right on the Embarcadero and proceed to finish the ride at Justin Herman Plaza, just west of the Ferry Building.

Opposite: Murphy Windmill, Golden Gate Park

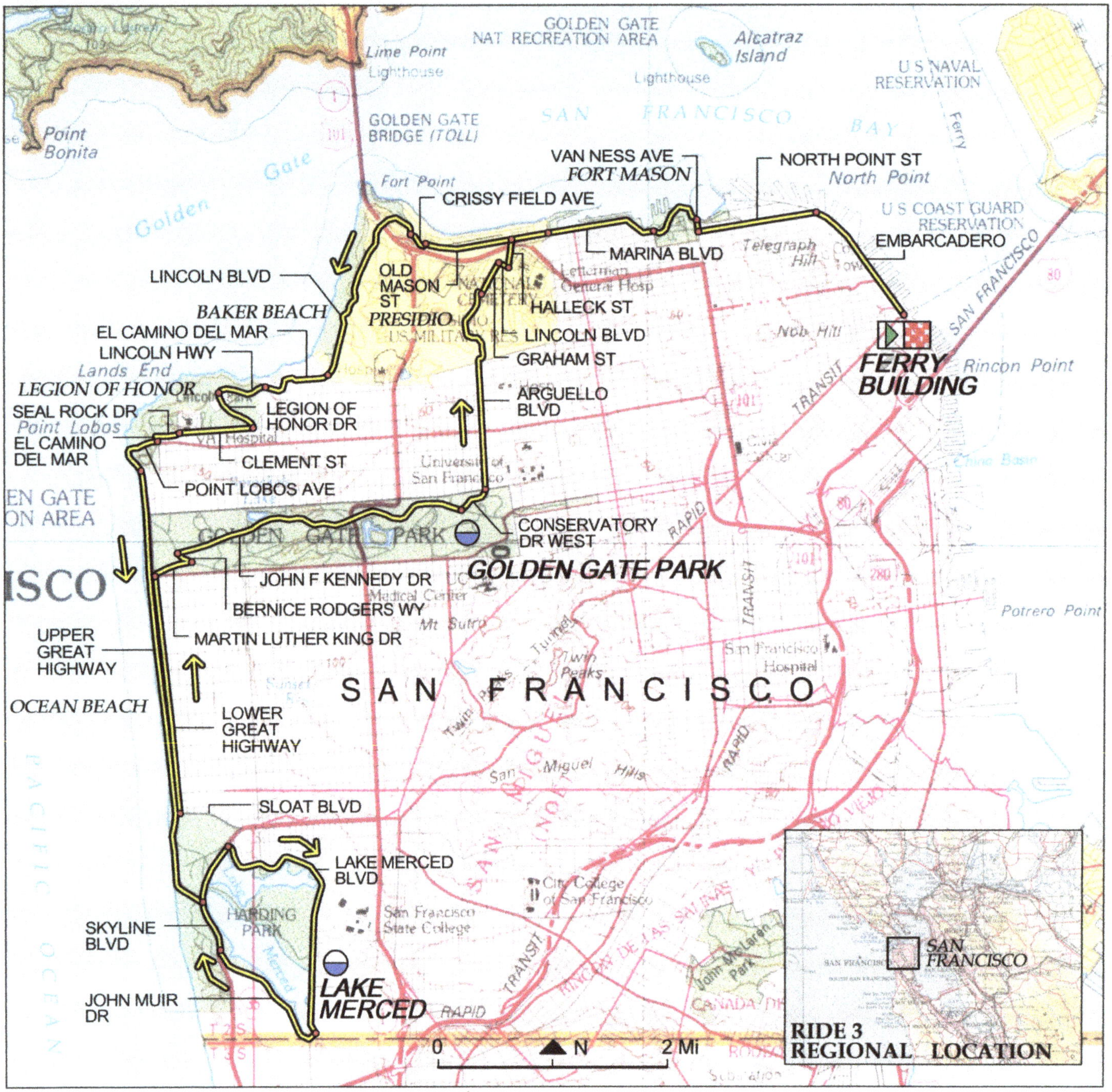

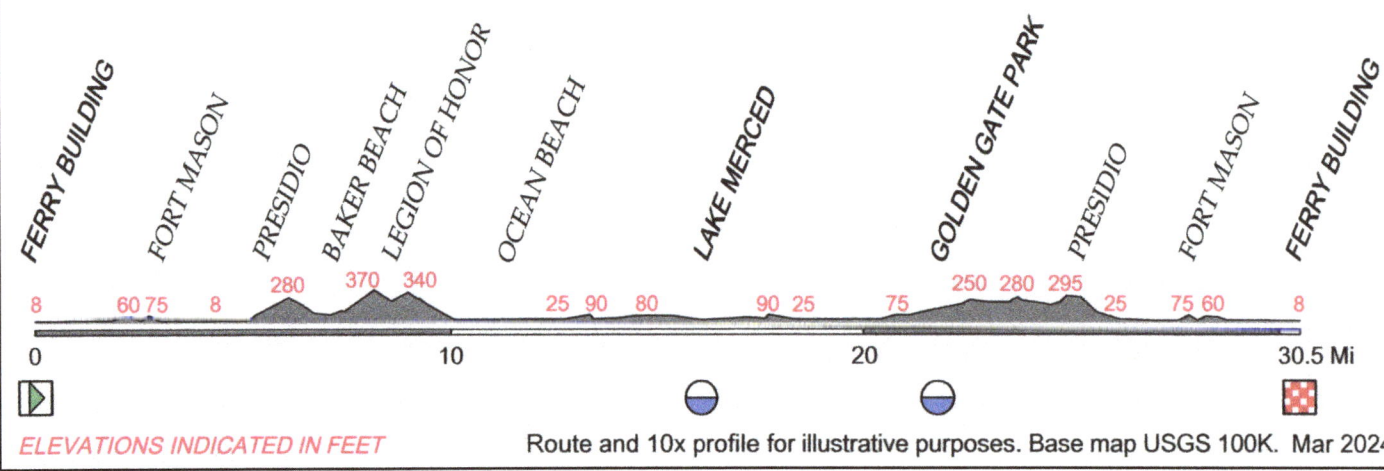

RIDE 3: LAKE MERCED / GOLDEN GATE PARK

ELEVATIONS INDICATED IN FEET

Route and 10x profile for illustrative purposes. Base map USGS 100K. Mar 2024

Ride 3: Lake Merced/Golden Gate Park

This ride can be considered as a 30 mile training route that extends the Ocean Beach ride by adding a loop around Lake Merced to the middle of the ride. Not quite as well known as the Golden Gate Park ride, this ride is mostly flat but includes about 1400 feet of climbing.

The route begins at the San Francisco Ferry Building and proceeds north and west along the Bay into the Presidio of San Francisco towards the Golden Gate Bridge — then through the Sea Cliff neighborhood and Lincoln Park, past the Palace of the Legion of Honor, the former Cliff House restaurant and along the Upper Great Highway past Ocean Beach to Sloat Boulevard. From there it continues south to Lake Merced, then circumscribes the lake in a clockwise direction before returning north on the Great Highway, through Golden Gate Park, the Presidio and along the City's northern waterfront to Justin Herman Plaza, at the

Lake Merced / Harding Park

foot of Market Street.

Ride Characteristics

Difficulty: Low

Distance: 30.5 miles

Terrain: Mostly flat, with several mild to steady uphill sections and short, steep climbing and descending sections within Fort Mason, the Presidio, and Golden Gate Park.

Elevation Range: Approximately 8 feet to 370 feet above sea level.

Climbing: Approx. 1460 feet

Situation: Urban and urban parkland setting.

Road Conditions: Street traffic and pedestrians, moderate to heavy; road surfaces, good to rough, slippery on foggy or overcast wet morning descents through wooded parklands.

Weather: Sea breezes off the bay and ocean can provide a substantial wind factor. Morning conditions can often be cool and cloudy.

Notes: Bike shops numbered 1 through 18 in Appendix 1 are found in the general vicinity traversed along this route through San Francisco. Nevertheless, shops are not always open or nearby — carrying essential tools, a pump, a tire repair kit and 2 tubes is recommended.

Approximate Ride Time: 2 hours.

Detailed Route Directions

Begin the ride in front of the Ferry Building and proceed north along the Embarcadero using the two-way, signed and green-painted bike lane. This lane is preferable for most cyclists, compared to the heavily-walked San Francisco Bay Trail segment located along the east sidewalk of the Embarcadero. The bike lane becomes one-way 'northbound' at Broadway. Continue in the bike lane to North Point Street. Use the signed and painted bike lane to cross the Embarcadero and turn left on to North Point Street. Ride along North Point Street, climbing steadily for two blocks at Columbus Avenue and continuing past Ghirardelli Square to Van Ness Avenue. Turn right on Van Ness Avenue and descend two blocks to its end, at the Aquatic Park Municipal Pier.

Turn left before the pier and ride into Fort Mason. The short climb up the former McDowell Avenue and around Black Point requires about five minutes of riding in a low gear or pedaling out of the saddle to gain about 65 feet of elevation. Watch for pedestrians and other cyclists walking bikes or those who stop along the San Francisco Bay Trail to view the Golden Gate Bridge. Other bicyclists may also stop suddenly on the steep incline after neglecting to shift into an easier gear. Still other cyclists may be descending rapidly from the opposite direction.

On a clear day, cyclists will enjoy stunning vistas of San Francisco Bay and the Golden Gate Bridge before descending past Fort Mason's Great Meadow to the pan-flat Marina Boulevard. This part of the route is just eight to ten feet above the bay's elevation. Proceed along Marina Boulevard past Gaslight Cove, the Marina Green and the St. Francis Yacht Club into the Presidio, where Marina Boulevard intersects Old Mason Street at Yacht Road.

Follow Old Mason Street west through the Presidio adjacent to the restored wetlands and Crissy Field, turn left and then quickly right on to Crissy Field Avenue and climb the short, steep pitch a few hundred feet to Lincoln Boulevard. Having gained about fifty feet of elevation, turn right at the stop sign and follow Lincoln Boulevard, climbing gradually past the Golden Gate Bridge and reaching an elevation of about 250 feet before descending through the western Presidio past Baker Beach. Climb gradually once again into the Sea Cliff neighborhood where Lincoln Boulevard intersects Camino del Mar at about 100 feet elevation. Continue west through Sea Cliff along Camino del Mar into Lincoln Park.

Once in Lincoln Park, the same road, now called Lincoln Highway, climbs steadily to the Palace of the Legion of Honor — the highest point of the ride — at about 350 feet elevation. South of the Legion of Honor, descend along Legion of Honor Drive to the intersection of Thirty-Fourth Avenue and Clement Street. Exit Lincoln Park and turn right onto Clement Street. Continue west, up the mild but steady incline to approximately 300 feet elevation at Forty-Sixth Avenue where Clement Street becomes Seal Rock Drive. Continue west on Seal Rock Drive and descend to Camino Del Mar. Turn left, continuing south one block on Camino del Mar to Point Lobos Avenue. Turn right on to Point Lobos Avenue.

Point Lobos Avenue presents a fast descent past the very popular Golden Gate National Recreational Area (GGNRA) Visitor Center and the former Cliff House restaurant. Watch for pedestrians, slow moving tour buses, cabs, and people backing out of the angled parking spaces along the seaward side of the street while proceeding south to the Great Highway just inland of Ocean Beach.

Lake Merced North / Skyline Boulevard

The next section is a straight, flat three miles, south along the upper Great Highway past Ocean Beach to Sloat Boulevard. Continue southeast on the Great Highway past Sloat Boulevard and over a short rise before turning left at Skyline Boulevard (Highway 35). Follow Skyline Boulevard a half mile or so to Lake Merced Boulevard, then turn right on to Lake Merced Boulevard.

Continue along Lake Merced Boulevard about two and a half miles — destination — John Muir Drive, This part of the course presents an odd combination of separated bike paths, bike lanes adjacent to high-speed 'boulevard' traffic and a segment near San Francisco State University where numerous motorhomes, RVs and campers are parked continuously for a half mile. The wider parked vehicles effectively eliminate a bike lane through this area, making it necessary to ride in one of the auto traffic lanes.

While California law certainly allows cyclists to use the full lane in this situation, it's best to do so with caution. This means proceeding along Lake Merced Boulevard as quickly

Lake Merced South / John Muir Drive

Conservatory of Flowers / Golden Gate Park

as possible, single file if in a group, from about Winston Avenue to Font Boulevard. After five minutes or so of potentially tense riding, a usable bike lane re-emerges and a gradual downhill continues to John Muir Drive.

Bear right on to John Muir Drive and begin the return ride by following the Lake Merced shoreline to Skyline Boulevard. Turn right and proceed on Skyline Boulevard to its intersection with the Great Highway. Use caution as you make the left turn on the Great Highway by crossing both northbound traffic lanes from the bike lane to enter the left turn lane. Make the stop, turn left, climb over the short rise towards the beach and continue on the Great Highway to Sloat Boulevard.

Ride east one block on Sloat Boulevard, to Forty-Seventh Avenue. After making a U-turn on Sloat Boulevard, proceed half a block and turn right on to the *lower* Great Highway. Ride along the lower Great Highway to Kirkham Street. At Kirkham Street, bear right on La Playa Street and continue north. Follow La Playa Street to Lincoln Way and cross into Golden Gate Park. Make the slight climb along Martin Luther King Jr. Drive to Bernice Rodgers Way. Turn left and ride a few hundred meters to John F. Kennedy Drive and turn right.

Continue through the park on John F. Kennedy Drive to the Conservatory of Flowers, turn left on Conservatory Drive West and climb the short rise to Arguello Boulevard. A short descent on Arguello Boulevard leads out of the park at Fulton Street.

Continue on Arguello Boulevard. North of Clement Street, Arguello Boulevard rises steadily, and then climbs abruptly for one steep block between Washington Street and Jackson Street, reaching an elevation of about 300 feet just south of the Presidio entrance. Once inside the Presidio, continue along a flat section of Arguello Boulevard, before descending rapidly to the Main Post at elevation 100 feet. Brake carefully and turn right on to Moraga Avenue at the bottom of Arguello Boulevard, then turn quickly left on Graham Street in front of the Presidio Officer's Club. Follow Graham Street to Lincoln Boulevard, turn right on Lincoln Boulevard and continue to Girard Road. Turn left on Girard Road which then becomes Marina Boulevard.

Continue east on Marina Boulevard to Fort Mason. Climb along the San Francisco Bay Trail through upper Fort Mason, past the Great Meadow and around Black Point, before descending to Van Ness Avenue and the foot of the Aquatic Park Municipal Pier. Climb gradually two blocks on Van Ness Avenue to North Point Street. Turn left and continue along North Point Street to the Embarcadero. Turn right on the Embarcadero and proceed to finish the ride at Justin Herman Plaza, just west of the Ferry Building.

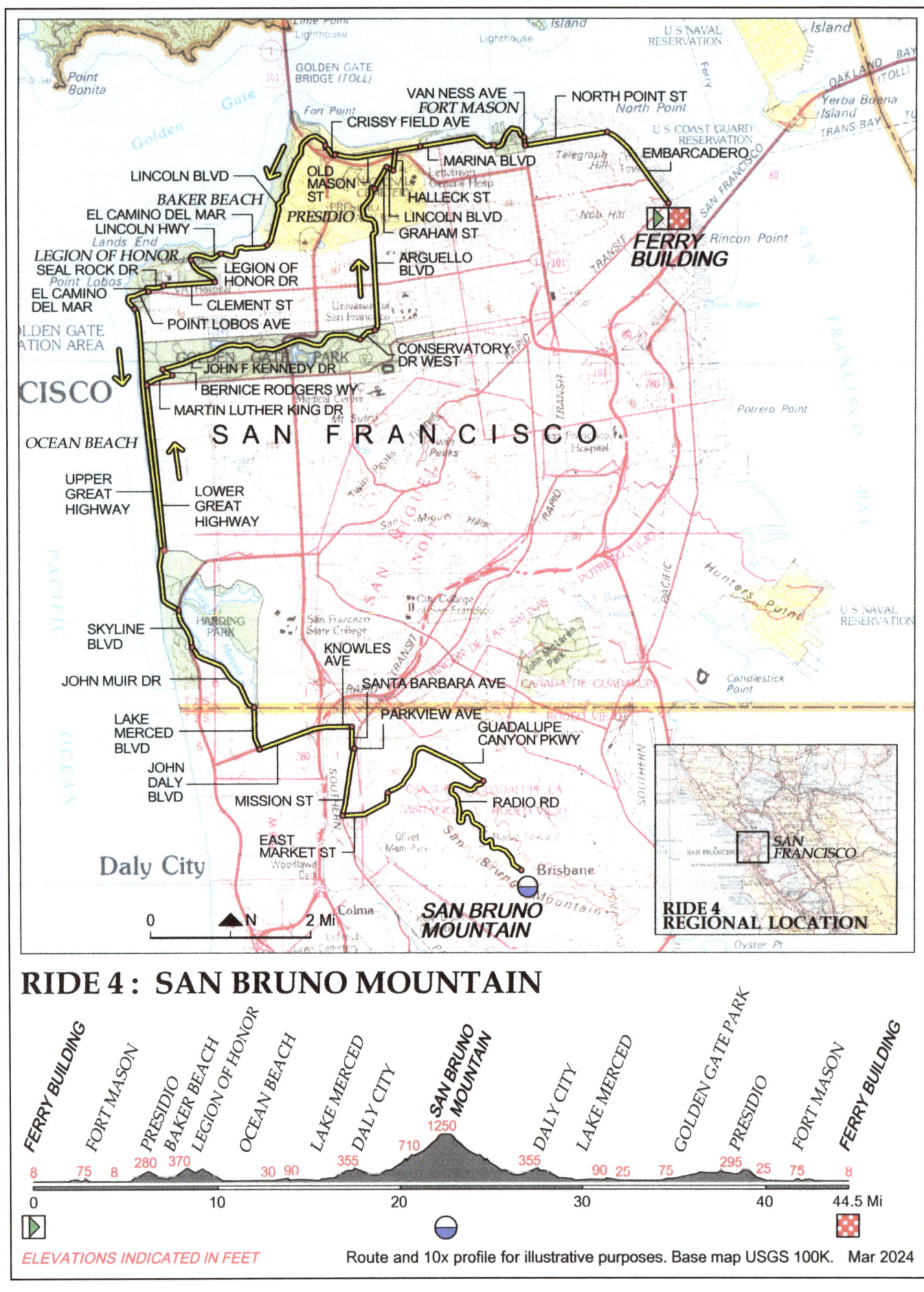

Ride 4: San Bruno Mountain

This 45 mile ride builds on the Ocean Beach and Lake Merced routes by adding the climb up San Bruno Mountain to the middle of the ride. The climbs are steady but not extremely steep or strenuous while the panoramic, clear weather views combined with a fast descent make it well worth the effort. The mountain's profile is a 'bell-shaped curve' with the return following a reverse of the outbound route. This middle-distance ride, with about 3200 feet of climbing, reaches the highest elevation in the northern San Francisco peninsula.

The route begins at the San Francisco Ferry Building and proceeds north and west along the Bay into the Presidio of San Francisco towards the Golden Gate Bridge — then through the Sea Cliff neighborhood and Lincoln Park, past the Palace of the Legion of Honor, the former Cliff House restaurant and along the Upper Great Highway past Ocean Beach to Sloat Boulevard. From there, it continues to Lake Merced and follows the south shoreline before reaching Daly City. A steady climb to the top of Mission Street in Daly City is followed by a speedy downhill and then the main climb on Guadalupe Parkway and Radio Road to the 1250 foot summit of San Bruno Mountain. The return follows a reverse of the outbound route to the coast, then proceeds along the Great Highway through Golden Gate Park, the Presidio and along the City's northern waterfront to Justin Herman Plaza, at the foot of Market Street.

San Bruno Mountain Panorama (North). Mount Tamalpais at horizon, downtown San Francisco at right margin

Ride Characteristics

Difficulty: Moderate

Distance: 44.5 miles

Terrain: Mixed, with flat sections, several mild to steady uphill sections and short, steep climbing and descending sections within Fort Mason, the Presidio, and Golden Gate Park. Three sustained climbs, on John Daly Boulevard and Mission Street in Daly City, and on Guadalupe Parkway and Radio Road leading to the summit of San Bruno Mountain. The return route includes a first, technical, then sinuous, four mile descent into Daly City.

Elevation Range: Approximately 8 feet to 1250 feet above sea level.

Climbing: Approx. 3175 feet

Situation: Urban and urban parkland setting.

Road Conditions: Urban street traffic, moderate to heavy; pedestrian traffic, light to heavy; road surfaces, mostly good to very rough on Radio Road atop San Bruno Mountain.

Sections of broken pavement with fallen Eucalyptus leaves, pods, and occasional branches require more caution, especially when descending in foggy or overcast wet slippery conditions through the wooded parklands.

Weather: Sea breezes off the bay and ocean, together with exposure at higher elevations can provide substantial wind factors. Morning conditions can often be cool and cloudy.

Notes: Bike shops numbered 1 through 18 in Appendix 1 are found in the general vicinity traversed along this route through San Francisco and San Mateo County. Nevertheless, shops are not always open or nearby — carrying essential tools, a pump, a tire repair kit and 2 tubes is highly recommended. This ride also includes segments of road where there are *no* services. If locked, an iron gate at the base of Radio Road requires a dismount in order to maneuver past the gate.

Approximate Ride Time: 3 to 3.5 hours.

Radio towers, San Bruno Mountain

Detailed Route Directions

Begin the ride in front of the Ferry Building and proceed north along the Embarcadero using the two-way, signed and green-painted bike lane. This lane is preferable for most cyclists, compared to the heavily-walked San Francisco Bay Trail segment located along the east sidewalk of the Embarcadero. The bike lane becomes one-way 'northbound' at Broadway. Continue in the bike lane to North Point Street. Use the signed and painted bike lane to cross the Embarcadero and turn left on to North Point Street. Ride along North Point Street, climbing steadily for two blocks at Columbus Avenue and continuing past Ghirardelli Square to Van Ness Avenue. Turn right on Van Ness Avenue and descend two blocks to its end, at the Aquatic Park Municipal Pier.

Turn left before the pier and ride into Fort Mason. The short climb up the former McDowell Avenue and around Black Point requires about five minutes of riding in a low gear or pedaling out of the saddle to gain about 65 feet of elevation. Watch for pedestrians and other cyclists walking bikes or those who stop along the San Francisco Bay Trail to view the Golden Gate Bridge. Other bicyclists may also stop suddenly on the steep incline after neglecting to shift into an easier gear. Still other cyclists may be descending rapidly from the opposite direction.

On a clear day, cyclists will enjoy stunning vistas of San Francisco Bay and the Golden Gate Bridge before descending past Fort Mason's Great Meadow to the pan-flat Marina Boulevard. This part of the route is just eight to ten feet above the bay's elevation. Proceed along Marina Boulevard past Gaslight Cove, the Marina Green and the St. Francis Yacht Club into the Presidio, where Marina Boulevard intersects Old Mason Street at Yacht Road.

Follow Old Mason Street west through the Presidio adjacent to the restored wetlands and Crissy Field, turn left and then quickly right on to Crissy Field Avenue and climb the short, steep pitch a few hundred feet to Lincoln Boulevard. Having gained about fifty feet of elevation, turn right at the stop sign and follow Lincoln Boulevard, climbing gradually past the Golden Gate Bridge and reaching an elevation of about 250 feet before descending through the western Presidio past Baker Beach. Climb gradually once again into the Sea Cliff neighborhood where Lincoln Boulevard intersects Camino del Mar at about 100 feet elevation. Continue west through Sea Cliff along Camino del Mar into Lincoln Park.

Once in Lincoln Park, the same road, now called Lincoln Highway, climbs steadily to the Palace of the Legion of Honor at about 350 feet elevation. South of the Legion of Honor, the road, now called Legion of Honor Drive, descends to the intersection of Thirty-Fourth Avenue and Clement Street. Exit Lincoln Park and turn right onto Clement Street. Continue west, up the mild but steady incline to approximately 300 feet elevation at Forty-Sixth Avenue, where Clement Street becomes Seal Rock Drive. Continue west on Seal Rock Drive and descend to Camino Del Mar. Turn left, continuing one block on Camino del Mar to Point Lobos Avenue. Turn right on to Point Lobos Avenue.

Point Lobos Avenue presents a fast descent past the very popular Golden Gate National Recreational Area (GGNRA) Visitor Center and the former Cliff House restaurant. Watch for pedestrians, slow moving tour buses, cabs, and people backing out of the angled parking spaces along the seaward side of the street while proceeding south to the Great Highway just inland of Ocean Beach.

The next section is a straight, flat three miles along the upper Great Highway past Ocean Beach to Sloat Boulevard. Continue on the Great Highway past Sloat Boulevard and over a short rise before turning right at Skyline Boulevard. Follow Skyline Boulevard to John Muir Boulevard. Turn left on John Muir Boulevard and proceed to Lake Merced Boulevard. Turn right on Lake Merced Boulevard and continue to John Daly Boulevard.

Turn left right on John Daly Boulevard and climb past the Highway 280 overcrossing and the Daly City BART Station to Knowles Avenue. Bear right on Knowles Avenue, climb one block, then turn right at San Diego Avenue. Proceed on San Diego Avenue to Parkview Avenue and continue on Parkview Avenue past Marchbank Park to San Diego Avenue. Proceed on San Diego Avenue to Citrus Avenue. Turn left and ride on Citrus Avenue two blocks to Mission Street (El Camino Real). Turn right and ride on Mission Street to Market Street. Turn left and follow East Market Street past Price Street, where it becomes Guadalupe Canyon Parkway.

Begin the steady two-mile climb up Guadalupe Canyon Parkway, first to the northeast and then following the topography to the entrance of San Bruno Mountain County Park. Turn left at the entrance and proceed past the gatehouse and through the parking lot to Radio Road. Begin the 1.6 mile winding 600-foot climb up Radio Road to the summit parking area at an elevation of about 1250 feet — destination and turnaround point of the ride. The actual peak of San Bruno Mountain sits just above 1300 feet elevation. The pavement is rough in places and it's an average 7% gradient whether spinning in a low gear or pushing a higher one. Nevertheless, it's actually a short climb with two switchbacks — the arrival comes after just half an hour or so of sustained effort! Car traffic on Radio Road is seldom an issue though there is a parking lot and trailhead access at the summit. Be aware — you may encounter an occasional car on the way up or down.

On a clear day make sure to take in the views all around as you are above most everything on the northern San Francisco peninsula. Begin the return by descending to the parking lot, keeping in mind that there are shaded sections of rough pavement and tree debris near the base of Radio Road. Heavy overcast and fog can also create wet and slick

Downtown San Francisco from Radio Road

conditions. Proceed through the parking lot to exit the County Park at Guadalupe Canyon Parkway. Turn right and descend along the winding Guadalupe Canyon Parkway.

Use caution but enjoy the freewheeling descent to East Market Street. Continue on East Market Street to Mission Street. Turn right and climb Mission Street steadily to Parkview Avenue. Turn left on Parkview and ride one block to Santa Barbara Avenue, then right on Santa Barbara Avenue and north to John Daly Boulevard. Turn left on John Daly Boulevard and descend rapidly, past the Daly City BART Station and Highway 280 overpass, to Lake Merced Boulevard. Turn right on Lake Merced Boulevard and continue to John Muir Drive.

Turn left on to John Muir Drive and follow the southern shore of Lake Merced to Skyline Boulevard. Turn right and continue on Skyline Boulevard to its intersection with the Great Highway. Use caution as you make the left turn on the Great Highway by crossing both northbound traffic lanes from the bike lane to enter the left turn lane. Make the stop, turn left, climb over the short rise towards the beach and continue to Sloat Boulevard.

Ride east one block on Sloat Boulevard, to Forty-Seventh Avenue. After making a U-turn on Sloat Boulevard, proceed half a block and turn right on to the *lower* Great Highway. Ride along the lower Great Highway to Kirkham Street. At Kirkham Street, bear right on La Playa Street and continue north. Follow La Playa Street to Lincoln Way and cross into Golden Gate Park. Make the slight climb along Martin Luther King Jr. Drive to Bernice Rodgers Way. Turn left and ride a few hundred meters to John F. Kennedy Drive and turn right. Continue through the park on John F. Kennedy Drive to the Conservatory of Flowers, turn left on Conservatory Drive West and climb the short rise to Arguello Boulevard. A short descent on Arguello Boulevard leads out of the park at Fulton Street.

Continue on Arguello Boulevard. North of Clement Street, Arguello Boulevard rises steadily, and then climbs abruptly for one steep block between Washington Street and Jackson Street, reaching an elevation of about 300 feet just south of the Presidio entrance. Once inside the Presidio, continue along a flat section of Arguello Boulevard, before descending rapidly to the Main Post at elevation 100 feet. Brake carefully and turn right on to Moraga Avenue at the bottom of Arguello Boulevard, then turn quickly left on Graham Street in front of the Presidio Officer's Club. Follow Graham Street to Lincoln Boulevard, turn right on Lincoln Boulevard and continue to Girard Road. Turn left on Girard Road which then becomes Marina Boulevard.

Continue east on Marina Boulevard to Fort Mason. Climb along the San Francisco Bay Trail through upper Fort Mason, past the Great Meadow and around Black Point, before descending to Van Ness Avenue and the foot of the Aquatic Park Municipal Pier. Climb gradually two blocks on Van Ness Avenue to North Point Street. Turn left and continue along North Point Street to the Embarcadero. Turn right on the Embarcadero and proceed to finish the ride at Justin Herman Plaza, just west of the Ferry Building.

Downtown San Francisco from Radio Road

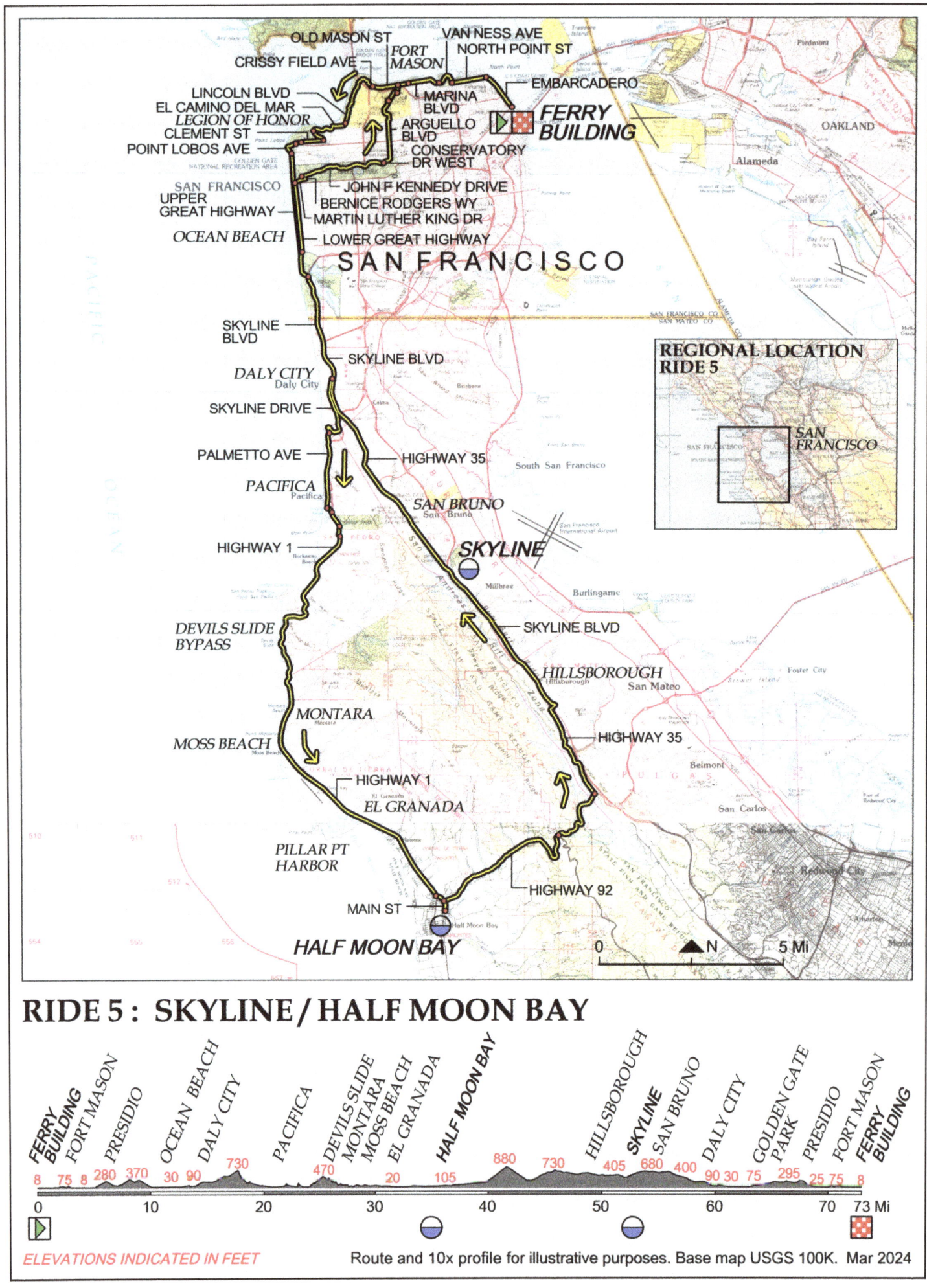

Ride 5: Skyline/Half Moon Bay

This ambitious, half-day commitment builds on the previous rides by adding a longer jaunt south along the rugged and scenic central coast, from San Francisco to Half Moon Bay and back — a distance of 73 miles with over 5000 feet of climbing. It's a challenging ride, even for fit cyclists, with several sections of sustained steep climbing, two-lane rural highways and intricate navigation through a number of cities and neighborhoods. However, the experience of cycling over thirty-six miles south along on one of the most renowned and picturesque segments of California's coast highway definitely qualifies as a major accomplishment and should be considered one of the Bay Area's middle distance signature rides, worth all of the multiple challenges and physical effort.

Similar to the Ocean Beach, Lake Merced and San Bruno Mountain rides, the route begins at the San Francisco Ferry Building and proceeds north and west along the Bay into the Presidio of San Francisco towards the Golden Gate Bridge —then through the Sea Cliff neighborhood and Lincoln Park, past the Palace of the Legion of Honor, the former Cliff House restaurant and along the Upper Great Highway past Ocean Beach to Sloat Boulevard. From there, it continues to Lake Merced and along Skyline Boulevard through Daly City, to Pacifica and Highway 1. The route follows Highway 1 over Devils Slide, through the communities of Montara, Moss Beach and El Granada to Half Moon Bay. Main Street in the center of town is the ride's halfway point and destination.

The return from Half Moon Bay climbs inland over Montara Ridge along Highway 92 and then parallels Highway 280, mostly on Skyline Boulevard (Highway 35), north to San Francisco. At Lake Merced the ride begins following a reverse of the outbound course to the coast, then proceeds along the Great Highway through Golden Gate Park, the Presidio and along the City's northern waterfront to Justin Herman Plaza, at the foot of Market Street.

Pacifica and Point San Pedro / Skyline Drive

Ride Characteristics

Difficulty: Moderate

Distance: 73 miles

Terrain: mixed flat and rolling, moderate and steady uphill with short, steep climbing and descending sections within Fort Mason, the Presidio, and Golden Gate Park. Four sustained steeper climbs, on Skyline Drive in Daly City, Devils Slide on Highway 1 just south of Pacifica, and Highway 92 east of Half Moon Bay. The rolling return route north along Skyline Boulevard includes numerous shorter rising sections and finishes with a five mile steady descent into Daly City.

Elevation Range: Approximately 8 feet to 880 feet above sea level.

Climbing: Approx. 5450 feet

Situation: Urban and urban parkland setting; rural segments of two lane highway.

Road Conditions: Street traffic and pedestrians, light to heavy; road surfaces, good to rough, slippery on foggy or overcast wet morning descents through wooded parklands.

Weather: Sea breezes off the bay and ocean, together with exposure at higher elevations can provide substantial wind factors. Morning conditions can often be cool and cloudy.

Notes: Bike shops numbered 1 through 23 in Appendix 1 are found in the general vicinity traversed along this route through San Francisco and San Mateo County. Nevertheless, shops are not always open or nearby — carrying essential tools, a pump, a tire repair kit, and 2 tubes is highly recommended, This ride also includes lengthy segments of rural road where there are *no* services.

Approximate Ride Time: 4 to 5 hours.

Detailed Route Directions

Begin the ride in front of the Ferry Building and proceed north along the Embarcadero using the two-way, signed and green-painted bike lane. This lane is preferable for most cyclists, compared to the heavily-walked San Francisco Bay Trail segment located along the east sidewalk of the Embarcadero. The bike lane becomes one-way 'northbound' at Broadway. Continue in the bike lane to North Point Street. Use the signed and painted bike lane to cross the Embarcadero and turn left on to North Point Street. Ride along North Point Street, climbing steadily for two blocks at Columbus Avenue and continuing past Ghirardelli Square to Van Ness Avenue. Turn right on Van Ness Avenue and descend two blocks to its end, at the Aquatic Park Municipal Pier.

Turn left before the pier and ride into Fort Mason. The short climb up the former McDowell Avenue and around Black Point requires about five minutes of riding in a low gear or pedaling out of the saddle to gain about 65 feet of elevation. Watch for pedestrians and other cyclists walking bikes or those who stop along the San Francisco Bay Trail to view the Golden Gate Bridge. Other bicyclists may also stop suddenly on the steep incline after neglecting to shift into an easier gear. Still other cyclists may be descending rapidly from the opposite direction.

On a clear day, cyclists will enjoy stunning vistas of San Francisco Bay and the Golden Gate Bridge before descending past Fort Mason's Great Meadow to the pan-flat Marina Boulevard. This part of the route is just eight to ten feet above the bay's elevation. Proceed along Marina Boulevard past Gaslight Cove, the Marina Green and the St. Francis Yacht Club into the Presidio, where Marina Boulevard intersects Old Mason Street at Yacht Road.

Follow Old Mason Street west through the Presidio adjacent to the restored wetlands and Crissy Field, turn left and then quickly right on to Crissy Field Avenue and climb the short, steep pitch a few hundred feet to Lincoln Boulevard. Having gained about fifty feet of elevation, turn right at the stop sign and follow Lincoln Boulevard, climbing gradually past the Golden Gate Bridge and reaching an elevation of about 250 feet before descending through the western Presidio past Baker Beach. Climb gradually once again into the Sea Cliff neighborhood where Lincoln Boulevard intersects Camino del Mar at about 100 feet elevation. Continue west through Sea Cliff along Camino del Mar into Lincoln Park.

Once in Lincoln Park, the same road, now called Lincoln Highway, climbs steadily to the Palace of the Legion of Honor at about 350 feet elevation. South of the Legion of Honor, the road, now called Legion of Honor Drive, descends to the intersection of Thirty-Fourth Avenue and Clement Street. Exit Lincoln Park and turn right onto Clement Street. Continue west, up the mild but steady incline to approximately 300 feet elevation at Forty-Sixth Avenue where Clement Street becomes Seal Rock Drive. Continue west on Seal Rock Drive and descend to Camino Del Mar. Turn left, continuing south one block on Camino del Mar to Point Lobos Avenue. Turn right on to Point Lobos Avenue.

Point Lobos Avenue presents a fast descent past the very popular Golden Gate National Recreational Area (GGNRA) Visitor Center and the former Cliff House restaurant. Watch for pedestrians, slow moving tour buses, cabs, and people backing out of the angled parking spaces along the seaward side of the street while proceeding south to the Great Highway just inland of Ocean Beach.

The next section is a straight, flat 3.5 miles along the upper Great Highway past Ocean Beach to Sloat Boulevard. Continue on the Great Highway past Sloat Boulevard and over a short rise before turning right at Skyline Boulevard (Highway 35). Follow Skyline Boulevard to its intersection with Westmoor Avenue. Turn right on Westmoor Avenue and proceed one block to Skyline Drive. Turn left on to Skyline Drive and continue climbing, then descending 600 feet or so into the coastside City of Pacifica.

Descend slowly to Westline Drive. Turn left on Westline Drive and continue to Palmetto Avenue. Turn right at Palmetto Avenue and continue through the Edgemar and Pacific Manor neighborhoods of Pacifica to the intersection of Palmetto Avenue and Clarendon Road, in the Sharp Park neighborhood. Turn left and follow Clarendon Road about 200 feet, then bear right on to Lakeside Avenue. Follow Lakeside Avenue to Francisco Boulevard, turn right and ride on Francisco Boulevard to Sharp Park Road. Francisco Boulevard becomes Bradford Way south of Sharp Park Road. Proceed on Bradford Way past Westport Drive and around the Moose Lodge, where Bradford Way becomes Mori Point Road.

Begin to follow the southbound bike path adjacent to Highway 1. The path becomes a highway bike 'lane' again at Rockaway Beach which continues over a hill to Linda Mar, then begins climbing steadily towards Devils Slide and the Highway 1 bypass opened in 2013. After many years in planning, twin bridges and tunnels were constructed here in order to realign the highway east of its original location along the face of the coastal bluff. Both northbound and southbound tunnels are lighted and equipped with separated bicycle lanes. Cross the southbound bridge and proceed with caution through the mile-long Tom Lantos Tunnel.

Devils Slide Trail

As alternative to transiting the tunnel, continue riding along the old Highway 1 alignment, which has been transformed into a paved segment of the California Coastal Trail. Opened in 2014, this mile-long segment is open to pedestrians and bicyclists and climbs to the crest of the Devils Slide before descending quickly to rejoin the existing highway just south of the tunnels. It's a short, steady uphill pull whether spinning a low gear, seated, or out of the saddle pushing a higher one — My experience, however, car traffic is nonexistent, there are working water fountains and bathrooms. Watch for the occasional skateboarder or Park maintenance vehicle on the Devils Slide trail.

Devils Slide Trail, South Entrance

The Devils Slide Trail is a great place to stop and enjoy the expansive views, stretching along the coast and west to the Pacific Ocean. Afterwards, descend to the southern trailhead and rejoin the existing highway. Continue south on Highway 1, another ten miles or so, through the communities of Montara, Moss Beach, and El Granada, past Pillar Point Harbor and Miramar, to the City of Half Moon Bay. Turn left where Highway 1 intersects Main Street and proceed on Main Street, over the Pilarcitos Creek Bridge and into downtown Half Moon Bay — destination point of the ride.

Grey Whale Cove and Devils Slide (at horizon) / Highway 1

After a rest break somewhere along the blocks of Main Street north of Correas Street, ride north on Main Street and begin the return. Cross the Pilarcitos Creek Bridge and turn right at the intersection of Main Street and San Mateo Road (Highway 92). Ride on San Mateo Road out of the City of Half Moon Bay, past the fruit stands and nurseries, to begin the five mile climb to the summit where San Mateo Road meets Skyline Boulevard (Highway 35). Climb steadily along Pilarcitos Creek and then more steeply as you make the switchback up the hill in the last mile or so. This is the highest elevation reached on the ride and a logical place to take a short break at the vista point where Highway 92 meets Skyline Boulevard.

The two mile descent along Highway 92/35 to the Crystal Springs Reservoirs is next. Now called Half Moon Bay Road, riders must invariably use maximum caution on the short but steep descent through the wooded watershed lands to the intersection of Highway 35 North and Highway 92. This section can be fast and fun if the level of auto traffic allows, however, like Highway 1, the shoulder along this section of highway is somewhat narrow and tree debris finds its way into the bike lane making it difficult to keep to the right and tense, especially when cars are maneuvering to pass. Wet and slippery conditions often complicate this descent. Courteous drivers will accommodate cyclists riding in the traffic lane around the tighter turns but watch your speed. Be aware of impatient drivers.

Montara State Beach / Highway 1

After crossing the dam that separates Upper and Lower Crystal Springs Reservoirs, turn left on Skyline Boulevard (Highway 35 *North*). Continue on Skyline Boulevard over the Skyline Dam and past the southern Sawyer Camp Recreational Trail entrance to Hayne Road. Turn right and ride on Hayne Road, underneath the Highway 280 overpass to Skyline Boulevard and Black Mountain Road, Turn left on Skyline Boulevard and continue, parallel to Highway 280, through the Hillsborough highlands to Trousdale Drive.

Cross Trousdale Drive and proceed on Skyline Boulevard, which merges briefly with Highway 280 here. Climb the gradual incline of the freeway on-ramp, and then ride in the highway bike lane north just a few hundred feet to the Millbrae Avenue exit. Leave the freeway and follow the off-ramp to the stop at Millbrae Avenue and Skyline Boulevard.

Cross Millbrae Avenue, and then continue on Skyline Boulevard to Larkspur Drive. Cross Larkspur Drive and continue on Skyline Boulevard, which again merges briefly here with Highway 280. Climb the incline of the on-ramp, then ride in the highway bike lane just a few hundred feet to the Skyline Boulevard exit. Take the exit, cross over the Highway 280 overpass and continue on Skyline Boulevard through San Bruno and into Daly City.

One last traffic challenge remains: negotiating the Highway 35/Highway 1 interchange at the crest of Skyline Boulevard, just north of Hickey Boulevard. The interchange is a classic freeway cloverleaf design requiring northbound cyclists to cross several on and off-ramps over the distance of about a half mile. The maneuver requires a cyclist's full attention.

At the intersection of Skyline Boulevard and Hickey Boulevard, Skyline Boulevard widens to four lanes and, just a few hundred feet further, becomes a divided highway. Cross Hickey Boulevard and continue on Skyline Boulevard, which quickly assumes the character of a freeway bike lane. *Two* lanes of vehicles to the left may be moving at fifty miles an hour or more as they approach the Highway 1 off-ramp. Bicyclists must move quickly across the two exiting auto traffic lanes when safe to do so, in order to remain on Skyline Boulevard. Make sure to be in a proper low gear, wait for an adequate break in traffic and ride quickly through the two exit lanes to the bike lane of northbound Skyline Boulevard.

Continue the gradual climb across the overpass within the bike lane. The peak of this last 'climb' of the day is about 500 feet up the road, however, not before another on-ramp brings auto traffic from Highway 1 onto northbound Skyline Boulevard. Watch for merging cars, cross the ramp lane and continue in the bike lane. After cresting the overpass, cross the second off-ramp — where cars exit from Skyline Boulevard to Highway 1 South. This off-ramp requires crossing a single lane. Auto traffic must slow down for a sharp turn — use caution and move quickly across to the bike lane of northbound Skyline Boulevard.

The last of the interchange challenges comes just another thousand feet further up the road where yet another on-ramp from Highway 1 merges with northbound Skyline Boulevard. Watch for cars accelerating downhill as they enter Skyline Boulevard. Cross the single lane on-ramp and continue in the bike lane.

Enjoy the ride's last sinuous 2.5 mile descent to John Daly Boulevard in Daly City but use caution — frequent wet, foggy, or windy conditions and heavy auto traffic can necessitate slower speeds on this sustained downhill. Continue on Skyline Boulevard past the Olympic Club, Fort Funston, and Lake Merced to the Great Highway. Use caution as you make the left turn on to the Great Highway by crossing both northbound traffic lanes from the bike lane to enter the left turn lane. Make the stop, turn left, climb over the short rise towards the beach and continue to Sloat Boulevard.

El Granada Beach Bike Path / Highway 1

Ride east one block on Sloat Boulevard, to Forty-Seventh Avenue. After making a U-turn on Sloat Boulevard, proceed half a block and turn right on to the *lower* Great Highway. Ride along the lower Great Highway to Kirkham Street. At Kirkham Street, bear right on La Playa Street and continue north. Follow La Playa Street to Lincoln Way and cross into Golden Gate Park. Make the slight climb along Martin Luther King Jr. Drive to Bernice Rodgers Way. Turn left and ride a few hundred meters to John F. Kennedy Drive and turn right. Continue through the park on John F. Kennedy Drive to the Conservatory of Flowers, turn left on Conservatory Drive West and climb the short rise to Arguello Boulevard. A short descent on Arguello Boulevard leads out of the park at Fulton Street.

Continue on Arguello Boulevard. North of Clement Street, Arguello Boulevard rises steadily, and then climbs abruptly for one steep block between Washington Street and Jackson Street, reaching an elevation of about 300 feet just south of the Presidio entrance. Once inside the Presidio, continue along a flat section of Arguello Boulevard, before descending rapidly to the Main Post at elevation 100 feet. Brake carefully and turn right on to Moraga Avenue at the bottom of Arguello Boulevard, then turn quickly left on Graham Street in front of the Presidio Officer's Club. Follow Graham Street to Lincoln Boulevard, turn right on Lincoln Boulevard and continue to Girard Road. Turn left on Girard Road which then becomes Marina Boulevard.

Continue east on Marina Boulevard to Fort Mason. Climb along the San Francisco Bay Trail through upper Fort Mason, past the Great Meadow and around Black Point, before descending to Van Ness Avenue and the foot of the Aquatic Park Municipal Pier. Climb gradually two blocks on Van Ness Avenue to North Point Street. Turn left and continue along North Point Street to the Embarcadero. Turn right on the Embarcadero and proceed to finish the ride at Justin Herman Plaza, just west of the Ferry Building.

Oppposite: Highway 92 (San Mateo Road)

Crossing the Golden Gate Bridge

Whether riding northbound into Marin County or southbound into San Francisco, crossing the Golden Gate Bridge by bicycle is complicated by the fact that there are two walkways, each used according to a specific schedule. The map/diagram found on page 42 depicts the bridge crossing alternatives.

Weekdays: East-Side Walkway

During daytime working hours on Monday through Friday, bridge workers use the west walkway exclusively. Consequently, cyclists traveling north and south must mix with pedestrians and use the east-side walkway.

Weekends: West-Side Walkway

On Saturdays and Sundays cyclists use the pedestrian-free, west-side walkway all day.

Northbound:

There are two alternatives for bicyclists crossing the Golden Gate Bridge northbound. Ride northwest along the Battery East Trail and follow the signs indicating directions to approach the Golden Gate Bridge's east-side or west-side walkways. Once across the bridge, Alexander Avenue and Conzelman Road connect to routes in Marin County.

Northbound Weekdays:

From the Battery East Trail turn left on to the short, switchback that leads directly to the east-side walkway. At the top of the ramp, turn right on the walkway and ride north across the bridge. Use caution and maintain a reduced speed — many walking sightseers cluster in various locations, especially near the south end of the walkway and around the bridge's towers. Other cyclists riding south are also weaving through pedestrian traffic. Be prepared for abrupt maneuvers when pedestrians and casual cyclists are present in large numbers.

Once across the bridge using the east-side walkway, follow the short ramp up to the Vista Point parking lot entrance/exit. Cross over and continue north on the separated bike path adjacent to the Highway 101 off-ramp, to northbound Alexander Avenue.

Northbound Weekends (and non-work weekday hours):

Continue west on Battery East Trail through the paved passageway underneath the bridge, to a paved segment of the California Coastal Trail just west of the bridge. Turn left and follow the Coastal Trail south one hundred feet, then make the sharp left turn on to the short, steep, paved connecting trail to the west-side walkway. Watch for southbound cyclists as you make another sharp turn left on to the bridge walkway itself.

Once across the bridge using the west side walkway, proceed northwesterly through the parking lot, up the short hill to Conzelman Road. Turn right and descend quickly to Alexander Avenue. Watch for cars accelerating southbound on to the Golden Gate Bridge and turn left on to Alexander Avenue. Ride north through the narrow highway underpass and past the Highway 101 north on-ramp.

Southbound:

There are also two alternatives for bicyclists crossing the Golden Gate Bridge southbound. Alexander Avenue and Conzelman Road provide approaches to the east and west-side walkways. Once across the bridge, the Battery East Trail and Lincoln Boulevard connect to routes in San Francisco.

Southbound Weekdays:

During daytime working hours on Monday through Friday, climb south on Alexander Avenue. Turn left on Alexander Avenue at the stop sign before the Highway 101 underpass and freeway on-ramp to Highway 101 north. Use caution and cross the northbound Alexander Avenue off-ramp and ride south in the bike lane on the separated bike path adjacent to the Highway 101 off-ramp.

Continue southbound in the bike path to the Vista Point parking lot. Cross the parking lot entrance/exit to a short ramp that leads directly to the east-side walkway.

After crossing the bridge using the east-side walkway, turn left and continue fifty feet to the short, switchback segment that connects to the Battery East Trail. Make the turn down the switchback, then turn right at the intersection and ride east on the Battery East Trail.

Southbound Weekends (and non-work weekday hours):

On weekends and during non-work weekday hours, climb west on Alexander Avenue, through the Highway 101 underpass to Conzelman Road, just before the Golden Gate Bridge southbound on-ramp. Watch for bad pavement while passing through the narrow tunnel and gear down properly before the short, but steep, 'one block' climb on Conzelman Road leading to the parking lot adjacent to the bridge. Turn left and proceed southeasterly through the parking lot to the west-side walkway.

Once across the bridge on the west-side walkway, slow down and watch for northbound cyclists as you make the 90 degree right turn at the end of the walkway. Descend along the short connecting trail to the California Coastal Trail and turn right, heading north just a few feet to the Battery East Trail. Turn right, pass through the short underpass beneath the bridge, then continue east on the Battery East Trail.

It's important to take it easy while crossing the bridge. It's dangerous to 'race' a bicycle across the east-side *or* west-side walkways. During the weekdays many walking sightseers cluster in various locations, especially near the south end of the *east-side* walkway. Other cyclists may also be riding in the opposite direction and weaving through pedestrians. Bicyclists must be prepared for abrupt maneuvers when groups of pedestrians or casual cyclists are present. Casual cyclists often stop suddenly and unintentionally impede other riders, especially around the bridge towers. Bay Area cyclists who ride the bridge regularly also know that the force of prevailing west winds on *both* walkways can make it difficult to maneuver around the north *and* south towers, whether or not pedestrians and other cyclists are present. Always use caution when crossing the bridge.

Crossing the Golden Gate Bridge (North Side)

Crossing the Golden Gate Bridge (South Side)

West walkway signage / Golden Gate Bridge

Golden Gate Bridge

RIDE 6 : MARIN HEADLANDS / RODEO LAGOON

ELEVATIONS INDICATED IN FEET

Route and 10x profile for illustrative purposes. Base map USGS 100K. Mar 2024

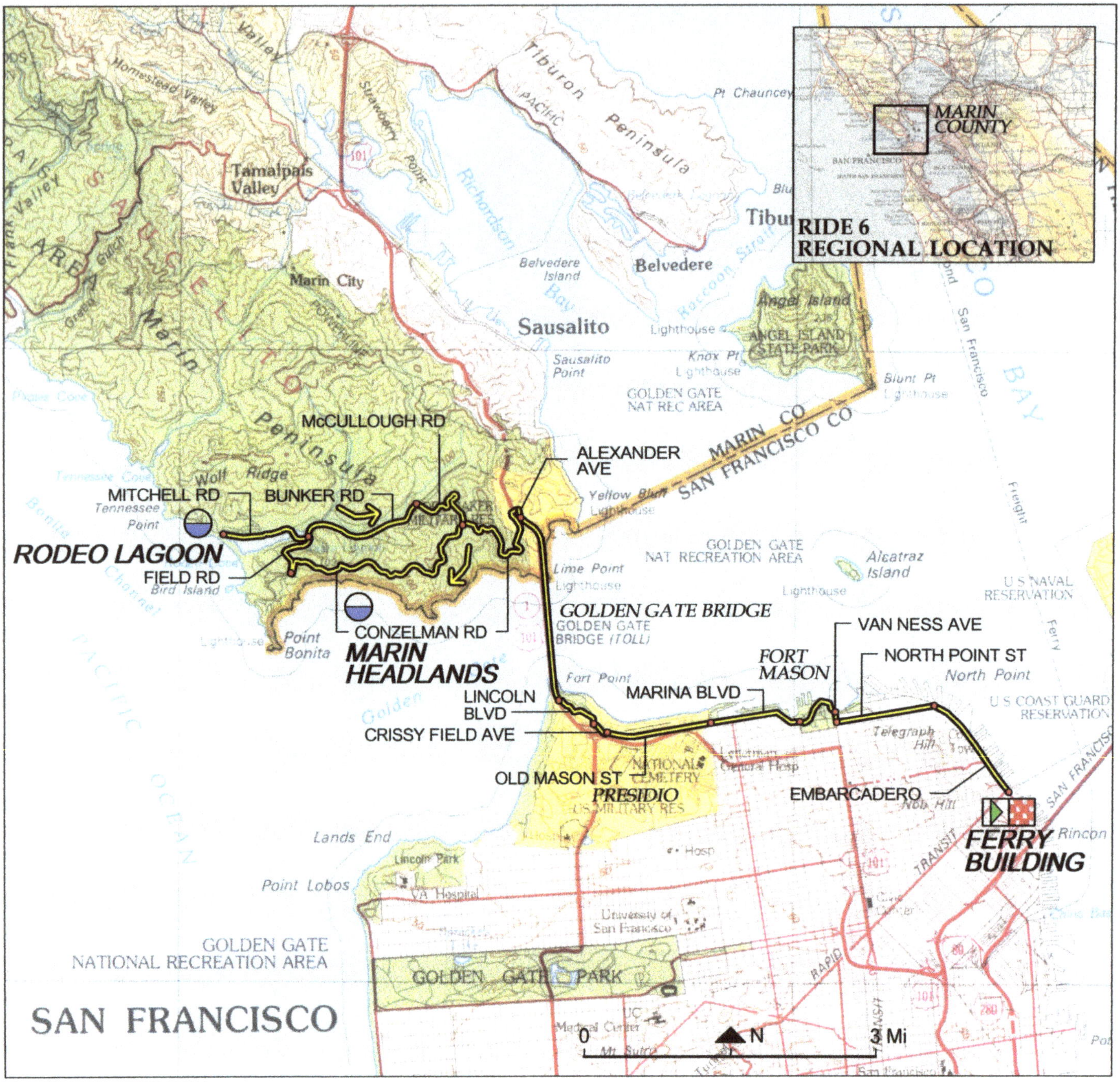

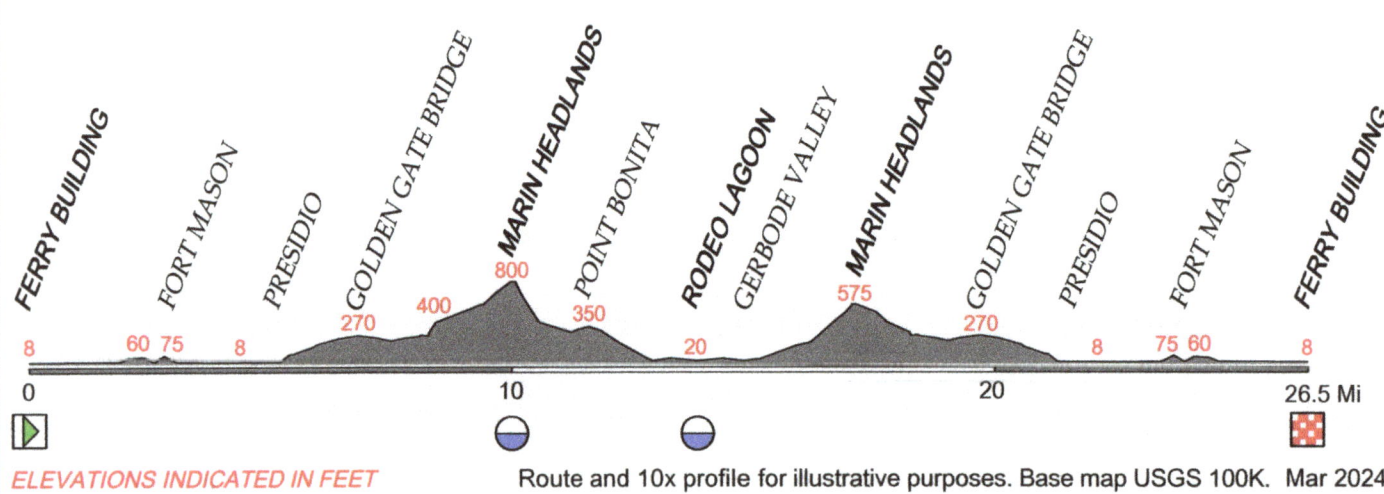

Ride 6: Marin Headlands/Rodeo Lagoon

This ride is a great short distance climbing workout in the Golden Gate National Recreation Area (GGNRA) of southern Marin County, just northwest of the Golden Gate Bridge. Cyclists from San Francisco, in training for any reason, have been known to make this roughly two-hour ride a daily early-morning routine. At a distance of 26.5 miles, it is the shortest of the 'climbing' rides, but nonetheless a notable Bay Area jaunt. On a clear day, stunning views of the Pacific Ocean, San Francisco and the Golden Gate, the Marin Headlands and Point Bonita, as well as those of Fort Cronkite and Rodeo Lagoon — combined with relatively car-free descents — make 1700 ft. of climbing worth the effort and the ride, a memorable one.

The route begins at the San Francisco Ferry Building and proceeds north and west along the Bay into the Presidio of San Francisco before crossing the Golden Gate Bridge. Riders then climb westerly along Conzelman Road through Battery Rathbone/McIndoe in the Marin Headlands and descend to Rodeo Lagoon and Fort Cronkhite. The course returns through the Gerbode Valley before a climb over the headlands to the Golden Gate Bridge. After crossing southbound, riders continue through the Presidio and along the City's northern waterfront to Justin Herman Plaza, at the foot of Market Street.

Golden Gate Bridge and San Francisco / Conzelman Road

Ride Characteristics

Difficulty: Moderate

Distance: 26.5 miles

Terrain: mixed, flat and gradual uphill sections with short, steep climbing and descending sections within Fort Mason and the Presidio. Two sustained, steeper climbs, up Conzelman Road to Hawk Hill, west of the Golden Gate Bridge, and up McCullough Road on the return leg of the ride. One *very* fast and steep descent west along the 7% grade, one way section of Conzelman Road through Battery Rathbone/McIndoe.

Elevation Range: Approximately 8 feet to 800 feet above sea level.

Climbing: Approx. 1700 feet

Situation: Urban and parkland setting; Bridge walkway; rural segments of one-way road and two-lane highway.

Road Conditions: Street traffic, moderate to heavy; pedestrians, moderate to heavy; road surfaces, good to rough, slippery on foggy or overcast wet morning descents through wooded parklands.

Weather: Sea breezes off the bay and ocean can provide a substantial wind factor. Strong winds from the west can make crossing the Golden Gate Bridge challenging, especially while maneuvering around the towers. Morning conditions can often be cool and cloudy.

Notes: Bike shops numbered 1 through 7 in Appendix 1 are found in the general vicinity traversed along the San Francisco part of this route, though not always open or nearby. No bike shops are located in southernmost Marin County — carrying essential tools, a pump, a tire repair kit and 2 tubes is highly recommended. This ride also includes segments of park road where there are *no* services.

Approximate Ride Time: 2 hours.

Detailed Route Directions

Begin the ride in front of the Ferry Building and proceed north along the Embarcadero using the two-way, signed and green-painted bike lane. This lane is preferable for most cyclists, compared to the heavily-walked San Francisco Bay Trail segment located along the east sidewalk of the Embarcadero. The bike lane becomes one-way 'northbound' at Broadway. Continue in the bike lane to North Point Street. Use the signed and painted bike lane to cross the Embarcadero and turn left on to North Point Street. Ride along North Point Street, climbing steadily for two blocks at Columbus Avenue and continuing past Ghirardelli Square to Van Ness Avenue. Turn right on Van Ness Avenue and descend two blocks to its end, at the Aquatic Park Municipal Pier.

Turn left before the pier and ride into Fort Mason. The short climb up the former McDowell Avenue and around Black Point requires about five minutes of riding in a low gear or pedaling out of the saddle to gain about 65 feet of elevation. Watch for pedestrians and other cyclists walking bikes or those who stop along the San Francisco Bay Trail to view the Golden Gate Bridge. Other bicyclists may also stop suddenly on the steep incline after neglecting to shift into an easier gear. Still other cyclists may be descending rapidly from the opposite direction.

On a clear day, cyclists will enjoy stunning vistas of San Francisco Bay and the Golden Gate Bridge before descending past Fort Mason's Great Meadow to the pan-flat Marina Boulevard. This part of the route is just eight to ten feet above the bay's elevation. Proceed along Marina Boulevard past Gaslight Cove, the Marina Green and the St. Francis Yacht Club into the Presidio, where Marina Boulevard intersects Old Mason Street at Yacht Road.

Follow Old Mason Street west through the Presidio adjacent to the restored wetlands and Crissy Field, turn left and then quickly right on Crissy Field Avenue and climb the short, steep pitch a few hundred feet to Lincoln Boulevard. Having gained about fifty feet of elevation, turn right at the stop sign and follow Lincoln Boulevard, past Long Avenue, climbing gradually to Battery East Road. Bear right on Battery East Road, which merges immediately with the Battery East Trail. Ride along the Battery East Trail and follow the signs indicating directions to approach the Golden Gate Bridge east-side or west-side walkways.[7] Watch for westerly winds, southbound cyclists and pedestrians on the bridge.

After crossing the bridge using the *west* side walkway, proceed through the parking lot, up the short hill to Conzelman Road. Turn left at Conzelman Road.

---

[7] Detailed instructions for crossing the Golden Gate Bridge, northbound, are included on page 40.

Opposite: Marin Headlands, Point Bonita and Rodeo Lagoon / Conzelman Road

From the *east*-side walkway, follow the short ramp up to the Vista Point parking lot entrance/exit. Cross over and continue on the separated bike path adjacent to the Highway on to Alexander Avenue at the stop sign, proceed through the short Highway 101 underpass and turn right on to Conzelman Road, just *before* the Golden Gate Bridge on-ramp. Watch for bad pavement while passing through the narrow tunnel and select a proper low gear before bearing right on to Conzelman Road, where a sharp rise immediately begins the steady climb along the headlands.

Conzelman Road is the main climbing part of the Marin Headlands/Rodeo Lagoon ride. After the first steep pitch, the grade becomes milder as you make your was past the vista points and traffic roundabout to the gated section of roadway. Weather permitting — there are also many great vistas along the next section which climbs to an elevation of about 800 feet. Once at the top, the road flattens and there is an opportunity to take some fluid and enjoy the views before beginning an exhilarating descent along the next section of Conzelman Road, through Battery Rathbone/McIndoe, a very steep, one-way road, carved into the slope of the headland.

There is no uphill auto traffic on the next section of Conzelman Road, a huge 'payback' for both the previous and subsequent climbing one must do during this ride. If you feel good, your bike is mechanically sound *and* if road and weather conditions allow, then this is a road where you can really 'let it out' on the downhill, particularly if there are no cars in front of you. But don't abandon all caution — this is a *very* steep descent with several very tight turns. Hard braking is necessary. Do *not* attempt to take these turns at high speed.

After the mile-long descent, continue on a flat section of Conzelman Road along Clydes Ridge that gradually descends towards Pt. Bonita. Turn right at Rathbone Road, then right again at Field Road. Follow Field Road downhill, past the Nike Missile Site, the Marin Headlands Center and the Headlands Center for the Arts to Bunker Road. Turn left on Bunker Road and ride across the Rodeo Lagoon bridge. Continue to Mitchell Road. Follow Mitchell Road past the Fort Cronkite buildings to the beach parking lot — destination and turn-around point of the ride — roughly 13 miles from the Ferry Building in San Francisco.

Begin the return by riding on Mitchell Road up the slight rise to Bunker Road. Continue on Bunker Road, cross Rodeo Lagoon again and pass Field Road. Follow Bunker Road through the Gerbode Valley and past the Presidio Riding Club stables before reaching McCullough Road. Turn right on McCullough Road and climb gradually, then steeply, eventually gaining about two hundred feet of elevation before reaching the roundabout at Conzelman Road.

Follow the roundabout counter-clockwise to the *left* and begin the descent to the Golden Gate Bridge on Conzelman Road. Use caution along this section — many driving tourists enter and exit scenic traffic 'pull-outs' and parking areas when stopping to view and photograph San Francisco and the Golden Gate Bridge.

During the weekends, descend to the Golden Gate Bridge parking area entrance, just above the base of Conzelman Road. Turn right and proceed through the parking lot to the west-side walkway. Watch for westerly winds and northbound cyclists on the bridge.

On weekdays, descend to the base of Conzelman Road. Watch for cars accelerating southbound on to the Golden Gate Bridge and turn left on to Alexander Avenue. Ride through the narrow underpass to the stop sign just past the Highway 101 north on-ramp. Use caution and cross the northbound Alexander Avenue off-ramp and ride along the bike path to the Golden Gate Bridge Vista Point parking lot. Cross the parking lot entrance/exit to a short ramp leading directly to the east-side walkway.[8] Watch for westerly winds, northbound cyclists and pedestrians on the bridge.

After crossing the bridge, follow the Battery East Trail to Lincoln Boulevard. Turn left on Lincoln Boulevard and ride to Crissy Field Avenue. Turn left on to Crissy Field Avenue and descend to Old Mason Street. Turn right and ride on Old Mason Street to Marina Boulevard.

Continue east on Marina Boulevard to Fort Mason. Climb along the San Francisco Bay Trail through upper Fort Mason, past the Great Meadow and around Black Point, before descending to Van Ness Avenue and the foot of the Aquatic Park Municipal Pier. Climb gradually two blocks on Van Ness Avenue to North Point Street. Turn left and continue along North Point Street to the Embarcadero. Turn right on the Embarcadero and proceed to finish the ride at Justin Herman Plaza, just west of the Ferry Building.

Gerbode Valley / Bunker Road

[8] Detailed instructions for crossing the Golden Gate Bridge, southbound, are included on page 41.

RIDE 7 : TIBURON PENINSULA

ELEVATIONS INDICATED IN FEET

Route and 10x profile for illustrative purposes. Base map USGS 100K. Mar 2024

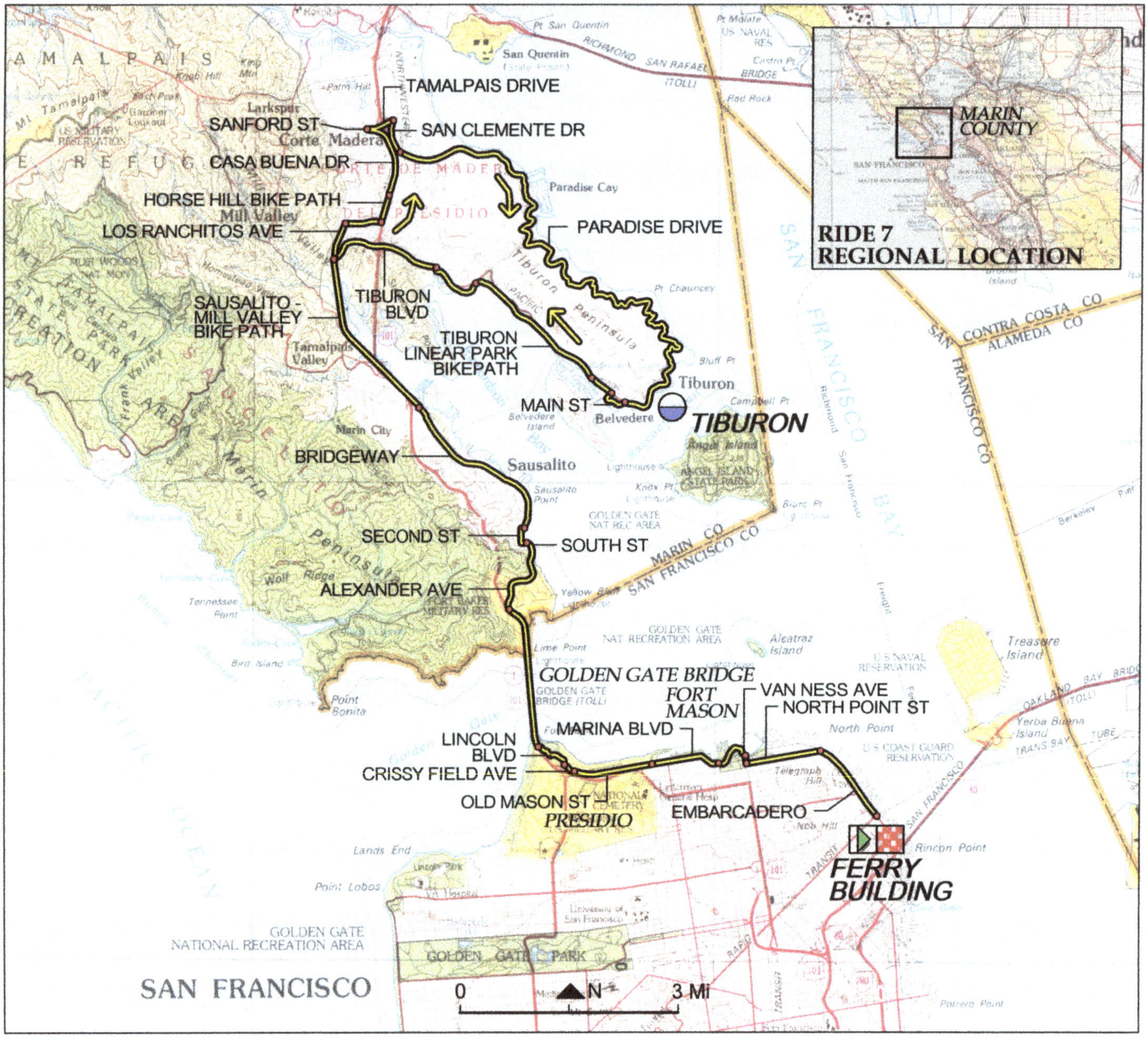

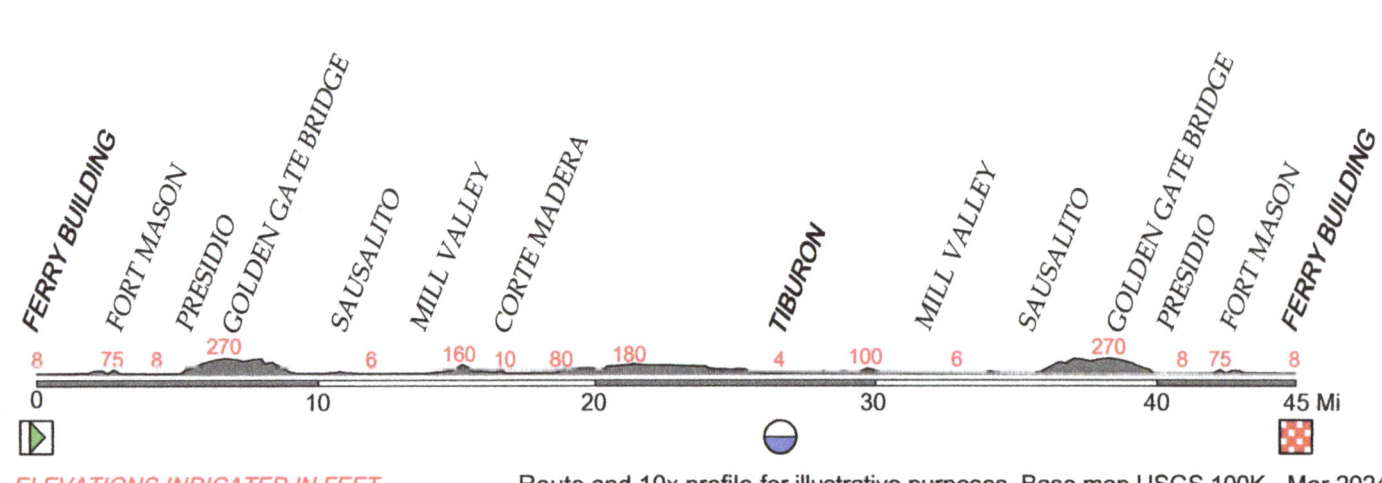

Ride 7: Tiburon Peninsula

This ride presents a middle distance, mostly flat ride through an urban but very picturesque bayside landscape in southern Marin County, following Paradise Drive — the perimeter road around the Tiburon peninsula. Casual cyclists and tourists often ride part of the 'Tiburon loop' course and return to San Francisco on one of the Sausalito ferries. Bicycling tourists and serious cyclists from San Francisco and beyond can usually complete the full ride in about three hours. At roughly 45 miles, it is one of the less difficult, medium distance rides and a well-known Bay Area favorite. The route profile is mostly flat and symmetrical with less than 1600 feet of climbing. After a flat two-mile section of bike path through Tiburon's linear waterfront park, the course returns to Mill Valley and then follows a reverse of the outbound route adjacent to Richardson Bay.

Riding in a clockwise direction around the perimeter of the Tiburon peninsula on a clear day provides spectacular views of the Bay, Angel Island, San Francisco and the Golden Gate Bridge. Even under overcast or foggy skies the broad views to the East Bay and south to San Francisco are impressive. Flat, separated bike paths combined with the relatively low level of auto traffic along Paradise Drive make this ride popular and well worth the effort.

The route begins at the San Francisco Ferry Building and proceeds north and west along the Bay into the Presidio of San Francisco before crossing the Golden Gate Bridge. Riders then descend into Sausalito and continue through Mill Valley into Corte Madera before beginning a clockwise loop around the Tiburon Peninsula following Paradise Drive.

The course returns from Tiburon to Mill Valley and Sausalito partly along 4.5 miles of flat bike path, follows the bay front through downtown Sausalito and then climbs to the Golden Gate Bridge. After crossing southbound, riders continue through the Presidio and along the City's northern waterfront to Justin Herman Plaza, at the foot of Market Street. Depending on time of day, the Golden Gate Ferry may provide an alternative for return from Sausalito to the San Francisco Ferry Building.

Ride Characteristics

Difficulty: Low

Distance: 45 miles

Terrain: mostly flat and gradual uphill sections with short, steep climbing and descending sections within Fort Mason and the Presidio. Includes a short, gradual northbound climb over the Horse Hill multi-use path transiting Mill Valley, a seven mile rolling section along Paradise Drive heading southeast above the bay shoreline towards Tiburon, and a sustained, gradual climb up Alexander Avenue from Sausalito to the Golden Gate Bridge on the return ride south.

Elevation Range: Approximately 4 feet to 270 feet above sea level.

Climbing: Approx. 1550 feet

Situation – Urban and urban parkland setting; Bridge walkway, paved multi-use paths, scenic segments of two-lane residential roadway.

Road Conditions: Street traffic and pedestrians, moderate to heavy; road surfaces, good to rough, slippery on foggy or overcast wet morning descents through wooded parklands.

Weather: Sea breezes off the bay and ocean can provide a substantial headwind wind factor, especially westbound or southbound on the bike paths directly exposed along the shoreline. Strong winds from the west can make crossing the Golden Gate Bridge challenging, especially while maneuvering around the towers. Morning conditions can often be cool and cloudy. Summer and Fall afternoon temperatures can be hot.

Notes: Several miles of flat, paved multi-use path. Expansive views of the central bay along Paradise Drive. Bike shops numbered 1 through 7 and 24 through 30 in Appendix 1 are found in the general vicinity traversed along this route through San Francisco and southern Marin County. Nevertheless, shops are not always open or nearby — carrying essential tools, a pump, a tire repair kit and 2 tubes is recommended.

Approximate Ride Time: 2.5 to 3 hours.

Detailed Route Directions

Begin the ride in front of the Ferry Building and proceed north along the Embarcadero using the two-way, signed and green-painted bike lane. This lane is preferable for most cyclists, compared to the heavily-walked San Francisco Bay Trail segment located along the east sidewalk of the Embarcadero. The bike lane becomes one-way 'northbound' at Broadway. Continue in the bike lane to North Point Street. Use the signed and painted bike lane to cross the Embarcadero and turn left on to North Point Street. Ride along North Point Street, climbing steadily for two blocks at Columbus Avenue and continuing past Ghirardelli Square to Van Ness Avenue. Turn right on Van Ness Avenue and descend two blocks to its end, at the Aquatic Park Municipal Pier.

Turn left before the pier and ride into Fort Mason. The short climb up the former McDowell Avenue and around Black Point requires about five minutes of riding in a low gear or pedaling out of the saddle to gain about 65 feet of elevation. Watch for pedestrians and other cyclists walking bikes or those who stop along the San Francisco Bay Trail to view the Golden Gate Bridge. Other bicyclists may also stop suddenly on the steep incline after neglecting to shift into an easier gear. Still other cyclists may be descending rapidly from the opposite direction.

On a clear day, cyclists will enjoy stunning vistas of San Francisco Bay and the Golden Gate Bridge before descending past Fort Mason's Great Meadow to the pan-flat Marina Boulevard. This part of the route is just eight to ten feet above the bay's elevation. Proceed along Marina Boulevard past Gaslight Cove, the Marina Green and the St. Francis Yacht Club into the Presidio, where Marina Boulevard intersects Old Mason Street at Yacht Road.

Follow Old Mason Street west through the Presidio adjacent to the restored wetlands and Crissy Field, turn left and then quickly right on Crissy Field Avenue and climb the short, steep pitch a few hundred feet to Lincoln Boulevard. Having gained about fifty feet of elevation, turn right at the stop sign and follow Lincoln Boulevard, past Long Avenue, climbing gradually to Battery East Road. Bear right on Battery East Road, which merges immediately with the Battery East Trail. Ride along the Battery East Trail and follow the signs indicating directions to approach the Golden Gate Bridge east-side or west-side walkways.[9] Watch for westerly winds, southbound cyclists and pedestrians on the bridge.

---

[9] Detailed instructions for crossing the Golden Gate Bridge, northbound, are included on page 40.

Once across the bridge, continue north from either walkway to Alexander Avenue. Follow the winding Alexander Avenue through the rolling terrain of Fort Baker, and descend into the City of Sausalito where Alexander Avenue becomes South Street. Continue on South Street to Second Street. Turn right on Second Street and ride to Richardson Street. Bear right on to Richardson Street, which becomes Bridgeway one block to the east.

Downtown Sausalito is completely flat and often full of walking *and* cycling tourists. The geographic setting along the bay is undeniably inviting. The weather can be warm and sunny when San Francisco is breezy, gray and foggy. Use extra caution along Bridgeway — pedestrians may cross the street mid-block or against traffic signals. Continue north through the city past the marinas and waterfront restaurants, Dunphy Park, and the Marinship area to Gate Six Road, just west of the houseboat marinas at Waldo Point.

Cross Gate Six Road and enter the Sausalito-Mill Valley bike path. Continue north on the flat 2.5 mile path, under the Richardson Bay Bridge, past Coyote Creek and the Bothin Marsh Preserve, to East Blithedale Avenue.

Cross East Blithedale Avenue and bear right on Lomita Drive. Continue on Lomita Drive which turns abruptly at the Edna Maguire Elementary School. Follow Lomita Drive and gradually climb to the short segment of paved bike path that continues over 'Horse Hill.' Ride along the path, climbing gradually to Casa Buena Drive.

Continue along Casa Buena Drive, past Marin Joe's Restaurant, to Sanford Street. Turn right on Sanford Street and immediately turn right again on to Tamalpais Drive. Climb over the Highway 101 overpass making sure to watch for cars accelerating towards the highway on-ramps. Continue on Tamalpais Drive and bear right on to San Clemente Drive. Continue on San Clemente Drive to Paradise Drive.

View north from Paradise Drive, Tiburon

Continue on Paradise Drive past Ring Mountain Preserve and up a short rise to begin a mostly flat and winding seven mile stretch of Paradise Drive. Enjoy the bay views to the east as this part of the course passes Paradise Cay and the Tiburon Romberg Center before eventually entering the City of Tiburon, on the southeast end of the peninsula.

Lyford's Tower / Paradise Drive, Tiburon

Downtown Tiburon is the destination point of the ride. Gone are the days when you could have coffee and pastry at the Swedish bakery, but the small plaza adjacent to Main Street is still a logical spot to stretch, or eat and drink something. Paradise Drive ends and intersects Tiburon Boulevard (Highway 131) at the roundabout adjacent to the west end of Shoreline Park near the Tiburon Ferry Landing. The return to San Francisco begins here.

Ride along Tiburon Boulevard past the main commercial district to Lagoon Road. Turn left on Lagoon Road, then immediately right to enter the Tiburon Linear Park bike path situated parallel to but between Lagoon Road and Tiburon Boulevard. Ride along the flat, two mile bike path enjoying the unobstructed views along the bay shoreline. This section can be especially breezy when westerly winds are coming off the bay, particularly in the late afternoon. Continue to the soccer (*futbol*) facility known as McKegney Field.

At the northern end of McKegney Field turn left where the bike path branches and descend towards the bay shoreline quickly following the path through a sharp right-hand turn and its merge with the wider Bay trail segment passing directly adjacent to the bay in front of the water treatment plant. Depending on the day and time, watch for pedestrians, pets, baby strollers, other cyclists, and the occasional water treatment plant vehicle, throughout this area. Continue towards 'Blackie's pasture,' cross the tidal inlet bridge, then bear left where the trail forks towards Greenwood Beach Road.

Turn left at the trail's intersection with Greenwood Beach Road and proceed through a short, *motor vehicle* barrier, to Greenwood Beach Road. Continue on Greenwood Beach Road past the Richardson Bay Audubon Center, where the road name becomes Greenwood Cove Drive. Continue on Greenwood Cove Drive to Tiburon Boulevard.

Turn left on Tiburon Boulevard and begin the gradual climb to the Highway 101 overpass. Continue over the overpass using caution — watch for cars entering the Highway 101 on-ramps. A turn signal just west of the overpass marks the end of Tiburon Boulevard and the beginning of East Blithedale Avenue.

After passing the turn signal, continue on East Blithedale Avenue to Ashford Avenue. Bear right on Ashford Avenue just before the Chevron gas station and continue four blocks to Lomita Drive. Turn left on Lomita Drive and ride to East Blithedale Avenue. Cross East Blithedale Avenue to enter the Mill Valley-Sausalito bike path. Ride south along the flat 2.5 mile path to Gate Six Road and Bridgeway, Sausalito's main street. Cross to the southbound bike lane on Bridgeway and continue through the city, climbing gradually past the Marinship area before descending into downtown Sausalito.

Continue on Bridgeway to begin the last leg of the ride, proceeding through Sausalito along the bay shoreline to Richardson Street. Bear right on to Richardson Street and climb one block to Second Street. Bear left on to Second Street and continue climbing several short blocks to South Street. Bear left on to South Street, ride one block and then climb the short, steep pitch where South Street becomes Alexander Avenue. Continue on Alexander Avenue climbing steadily past East Road and Danes Drive in Fort Baker.

Climb on Alexander Avenue to the east-side or west-side Golden Gate Bridge walkway.[10] Watch for westerly winds, northbound cyclists and pedestrians on the bridge. After crossing the bridge, follow the Battery East Trail to Lincoln Boulevard. Turn left on Lincoln Boulevard and ride to Crissy Field Avenue. Turn left on to Crissy Field Avenue and descend to Old Mason Street. Turn right and ride on Old Mason Street to Marina Boulevard.

Continue east on Marina Boulevard to Fort Mason. Climb along the San Francisco Bay Trail through upper Fort Mason, past the Great Meadow and around Black Point, before descending to Van Ness Avenue and the foot of the Aquatic Park Municipal Pier. Climb gradually two blocks on Van Ness Avenue to North Point Street. Turn left and continue along North Point Street to the Embarcadero. Turn right on the Embarcadero and proceed to finish the ride at Justin Herman Plaza, just west of the Ferry Building.

Tiburon waterfront bike path with Mount Tamalpais in the distance

---

[10] Detailed instructions for crossing the Golden Gate Bridge, southbound, are included on page 41.

RIDE 8 : MOUNT TAMALPAIS

ELEVATIONS INDICATED IN FEET

Route and 10x profile for illustrative purposes. Base map USGS 100K. Mar 2024

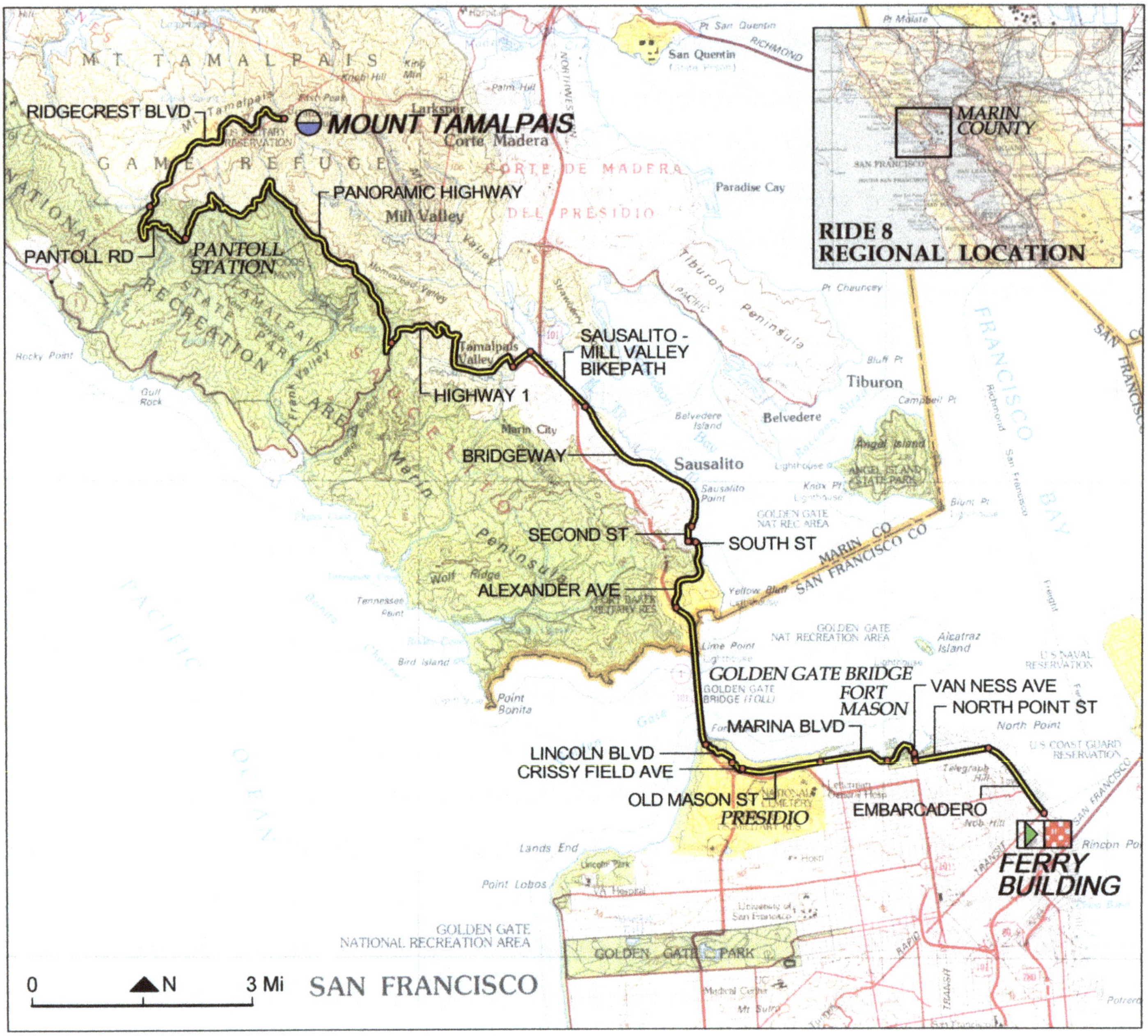

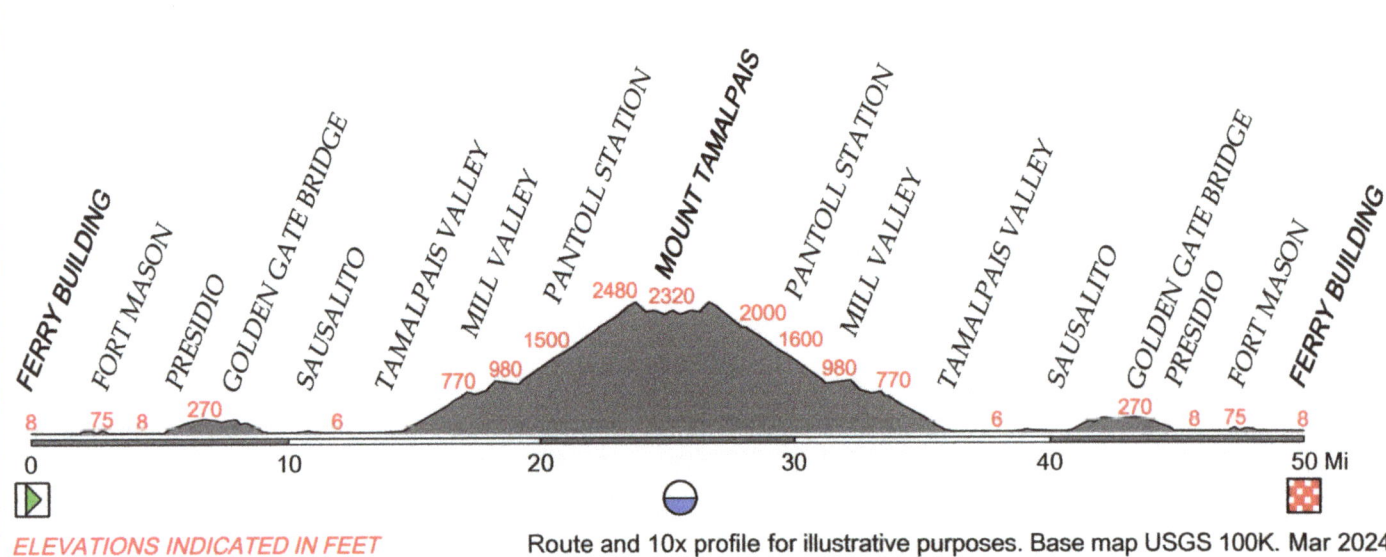

Ride 8: Mount Tamalpais

This ride presents a middle distance, sustained climb through the urban and adjacent parkland and mountain landscape of southern Marin County. At 2670 feet elevation, Mount Tamalpais is one of the highest peaks around the Bay and part of a trio of the San Francisco region's steepest and most challenging climbs.[11] The ride, itself, reaches 2480 feet but whether undertaken as a recreational ride or as training, this one is strenuous — typically taking a fit rider over three hours to complete the climb and return to San Francisco.

Some sustained effort is required on the steeper parts of the climb but there are also flatter and gently-rising sections where cyclists may glimpse the picturesque redwood forest and beautiful clear weather views of the Pacific Ocean, southern Marin County, San Francisco, and the East Bay. At 50 miles, it is a tough, medium distance ride and another local 'favorite,' requiring almost 4000 feet of climbing. Depending on the amount of auto traffic, the steep, technical descent can be speedy or slow, exhilarating or nerve wracking but still a worthwhile part of the challenge. Some cyclists make this ride a regular workout — others approach it as a high-level onetime achievement.

The route begins at the San Francisco Ferry Building and proceeds north and west along the Bay into the Presidio of San Francisco before crossing the Golden Gate Bridge. Riders then descend into Sausalito and continue to Tamalpais Valley Junction, where the Highway One climb to the Panoramic Highway and Pantoll Station begins. Steady climbing continues along Pantoll Road to Rock Springs,[12] past the Mountain Theatre and along Ridgecrest Boulevard to the summit parking area below the East Peak of Mount Tamalpais.

The Mount Tamalpais ride is an 'out and back' course. The route profile is a classic 'bell-shaped curve' — the return follows the reverse of the outbound route. The return begins with a short climb, followed by a steady, sometimes steep, descent through the State Park along Ridgecrest Boulevard and Pantoll Road, to Panoramic Highway. The mostly 'downhill' Panoramic Highway reaches Highway 1, which leads to Tamalpais Valley Junction.

The route continues to Sausalito along a 1.5 mile segment of flat bike path, follows the bay front through town and then climbs to the Golden Gate Bridge. After crossing southbound, riders continue through the Presidio and along the City's northern waterfront to Justin Herman Plaza, at the foot of Market Street. Depending on time of day, the Golden Gate Ferry may provide an alternative for return from Sausalito to the San Francisco Ferry Building.

Ride Characteristics

Difficulty: High

Distance: 50 miles

Terrain: Mixed flat and hilly, with short, steep climbing and descending sections within Fort Mason and the Presidio, preceding the sustained, moderate and steep 11.5 mile climb to the top of Mount Tamalpais. Steady, steep and rolling descent on the return to Tamalpais Valley Junction.

Elevation Range: Approximately 5 feet to 2480 feet above sea level.

---

[11] See Ride 14 - Mount Diablo (elev. 3850 ft.) and Ride 16 – Mount Hamilton (elev. 4220 ft.).
[12] Elevation 2070 feet.

Climbing: Approx. 3970 feet
Situation: Urban and parkland setting; Bridge walkway; rural segments of two lane highway.
Road Conditions: Street traffic and pedestrians, moderate to heavy; road surfaces, good to rough, slippery on foggy or overcast wet morning descents through wooded parklands.
Weather: Sea breezes off the bay and ocean can provide a substantial wind factor. Strong winds from the west can make crossing the Golden Gate Bridge challenging, especially while maneuvering around the towers. Morning conditions can often be cool and cloudy. Summer and Fall afternoon temperatures can be hot.
Notes: Bike shops numbered 1 through 7 and 24 through 27 in Appendix 1 are found in the general vicinity traversed along this route through San Francisco and Marin County. Nevertheless, shops are not always open or nearby — carrying essential tools, a pump, a tire repair kit and 2 tubes is highly recommended. This ride also includes significant segments of park road where there are *no* services.
Approximate Ride Time: 3 to 4 hours.

Detailed Route Directions

Begin the ride in front of the Ferry Building and proceed north along the Embarcadero using the two-way, signed and green-painted bike lane. This lane is preferable for most cyclists, compared to the heavily-walked San Francisco Bay Trail segment located along the east sidewalk of the Embarcadero. The bike lane becomes one-way 'northbound' at Broadway. Continue in the bike lane to North Point Street. Use the signed and painted bike lane to cross the Embarcadero and turn left on to North Point Street. Ride along North Point Street, climbing steadily for two blocks at Columbus Avenue and continuing past Ghirardelli Square to Van Ness Avenue. Turn right on Van Ness Avenue and descend two blocks to its end, at the Aquatic Park Municipal Pier.

Turn left before the pier and ride into Fort Mason. The short climb up the former McDowell Avenue and around Black Point requires about five minutes of riding in a low gear or pedaling out of the saddle to gain about 65 feet of elevation. Watch for pedestrians and other cyclists walking bikes or those who stop along the San Francisco Bay Trail to view the Golden Gate Bridge. Other bicyclists may also stop suddenly on the steep incline after neglecting to shift into an easier gear. Still other cyclists may be descending rapidly from the opposite direction.

On a clear day, cyclists will enjoy stunning vistas of San Francisco Bay and the Golden Gate Bridge before descending past Fort Mason's Great Meadow to the pan-flat Marina Boulevard. This part of the route is just eight to ten feet above the bay's elevation. Proceed along Marina Boulevard past Gaslight Cove, the Marina Green and the St. Francis Yacht Club into the Presidio, where Marina Boulevard intersects Old Mason Street at Yacht Road.

Follow Old Mason Street through the Presidio adjacent to the restored wetlands and Crissy Field, turn left and then quickly right on Crissy Field Avenue and climb the short, steep pitch a few hundred feet to Lincoln Boulevard. Having gained about fifty feet of elevation, turn right at the stop sign and follow Lincoln Boulevard, past Long Avenue, climbing gradually to Battery East Road. Bear right on Battery East Road, which merges immediately with the Battery East Trail. Ride along the Battery East Trail and follow the signs indicating directions to approach the Golden Gate Bridge's east-side or west-side walkways.[13] Watch

---

[13] Detailed instructions for crossing the Golden Gate Bridge, northbound, are included on page 40.

for westerly winds, southbound cyclists and pedestrians on the bridge.

Once across the bridge, continue north from either walkway to Alexander Avenue. Follow the winding Alexander Avenue through the rolling terrain of Fort Baker, and descend into the City of Sausalito where Alexander Avenue becomes South Street. Continue on South Street to Second Street. Turn right on to Second Street and ride to Richardson Street. Bear right on to Richardson Street, which becomes Bridgeway one block to the east.

Downtown Sausalito is completely flat and often full of walking *and* cycling tourists. The geographic setting along the bay is undeniably inviting. The weather can be warm and sunny when San Francisco is breezy, gray and foggy. Use extra caution along Bridgeway — pedestrians may cross the street mid-block or against traffic signals. Continue north through the city past the marinas and waterfront restaurants, Dunphy Park, and the Marinship area to Gate Six Road, just west of the houseboat marinas at Waldo Point.

Cross Gate Six Road and enter the Sausalito-Mill Valley bike path. Continue north on the path about a mile to its intersection with the Coyote Creek bike path, which connects west to Tamalpais Valley Junction. Turn left and follow the flat path adjacent to Coyote Creek, less than a half-mile, to Highway 1 in Tamalpais Valley Junction. Turn right onto Highway 1 and continue another quarter-mile to reach its intersection with Almonte Boulevard.

Turn left at Almonte Boulevard to remain on Highway 1 and begin the ride's first serious climbing. Continue along Highway 1 steadily gaining about 700 feet of elevation before the road levels off near Panoramic Highway. Shift to a low gear and bear right on Panoramic Highway. Once beyond the first short rise remain in a very low gear and climb the steep, tight, hairpin turn that follows, quickly gaining about 20-30 feet of elevation in just a hundred feet of road distance. Ride along the next flatter section of Panoramic Highway to its intersection with Sequoia Valley Road and Muir Woods Road.[14]

Continue on Panoramic Highway past Sequoia Valley Road and Muir Woods Road, beginning the second steeper section, climbing to an elevation of about 1000 feet at Mountain Home Inn. Ride into Mount Tamalpais State Park and follow Panoramic Highway as it climbs another 500 feet to Pantoll Station.[15] Several switchback turns along the way require shifting to a low gear and/or pedaling while riding 'out of the saddle.'

After this steady climbing section, bear right on to Pantoll Road, where the road flattens out briefly. A third section of steady climbing on Pantoll Road soon follows, before reaching Ridgecrest Boulevard and the Rock Springs parking lot.[16]

At Rock Springs, turn right on to Ridgecrest Boulevard and continue climbing past the Mountain Theatre and past West Peak to finish this major feat at the State Park's East Peak parking lot — elevation about 2500 feet — destination and turnaround point for the ride.

Most cyclists will stretch a bit and eat/drink something while off the bike, taking a well-deserved break at the vista point. Mount Tamalpais is the *halfway* point in the ride — there's a lot of 'downhill' to come but there are still 25 miles to ride before reaching the Ferry Building in San Francisco. Take it easy while descending along Ridgecrest Boulevard. Several hiking trails cross the road just west of the parking lot.

The return ride follows the earlier mountain-bound directions in reverse order. The downhill from the parking lot quickly becomes a climb back over West Peak before cyclists

---

[14] Also known as 'Four Corners.'
[15] Elevation 1500 feet.
[16] Elevation 2070 feet.

Approaching Pantoll Station / Panoramic Highway

can begin descending in earnest. Continue down Ridgecrest Boulevard to its intersection with Pantoll Road at Rock Springs parking lot before turning left on Pantoll Road and riding to its intersection with Panoramic Highway. Use caution and cross from Pantoll Road into the east bound lane of Panoramic Highway. Descend through several steep switchback turns, past Rattlesnake Creek and Fern Creek, to the Mountain Home Inn.

At Mountain Home Inn begin the short, steady climb to the Ranger Station, then descend again further to 'Four Corners,' the intersection of Panoramic Highway with Sequoia Valley Road and Muir Woods Road. Continue southbound on Panoramic Highway where you will climb gradually and then descend quickly into the very tight 'hairpin' turn where Panoramic Highway reverses direction and intersects Highway 1. Turn left at the intersection and begin the descent along Highway 1 to Tamalpais Valley Junction.

Turn right at the intersection of Almonte Boulevard and Highway 1 and continue on Highway 1, less than a quarter-mile, to the Coyote Creek bike path. Bear right onto the path and ride east, about a half-mile, to the Mill Valley-Sausalito bike path. Turn right and ride south along the one-mile segment to Gate Six Road and Bridgeway, Sausalito's main street. Cross to the southbound bike lane on Bridgeway and continue through the city, climbing gradually past the Marinship area before descending into downtown Sausalito.

Continue on Bridgeway to begin the last leg of the ride, proceeding through Sausalito along the bay shoreline to Richardson Street. Bear right on to Richardson Street and climb one block to Second Street. Bear left on to Second Street and continue climbing several short blocks to South Street. Bear left on to South Street, ride one block and then climb the short, steep pitch where South Street becomes Alexander Avenue. Continue on Alexander Avenue climbing steadily past East Road and Danes Drive in Fort Baker.

Climb on Alexander Avenue to the east-side or west-side Golden Gate Bridge walkway[17] Watch for westerly winds, northbound cyclists and pedestrians on the bridge. After crossing the bridge, follow the Battery East Trail to Lincoln Boulevard. Turn left on Lincoln Boulevard and ride to Crissy Field Avenue. Turn left on to Crissy Field Avenue and descend to Old Mason Street. Turn right and ride on Old Mason Street to Marina Boulevard.

Continue east on Marina Boulevard to Fort Mason. Climb along the San Francisco Bay Trail through upper Fort Mason, past the Great Meadow and around Black Point, before descending to Van Ness Avenue and the foot of the Aquatic Park Municipal Pier. Climb gradually two blocks on Van Ness Avenue to North Point Street. Turn left and continue along North Point Street to the Embarcadero. Turn right on the Embarcadero and proceed to finish the ride at Justin Herman Plaza, just west of the Ferry Building.

Mount Tamalpais Summit Panorama (South). Mount Diablo (l), Tiburon Peninsula (c) and San Francisco (r) in view at horizon

---

[17] Detailed instructions for crossing the Golden Gate Bridge, southbound, are included on page 41.

RIDE 9 : STINSON BEACH / MUIR BEACH

ELEVATIONS INDICATED IN FEET

Route and 10x profile for illustrative purposes. Base map USGS 100K. Mar 2024

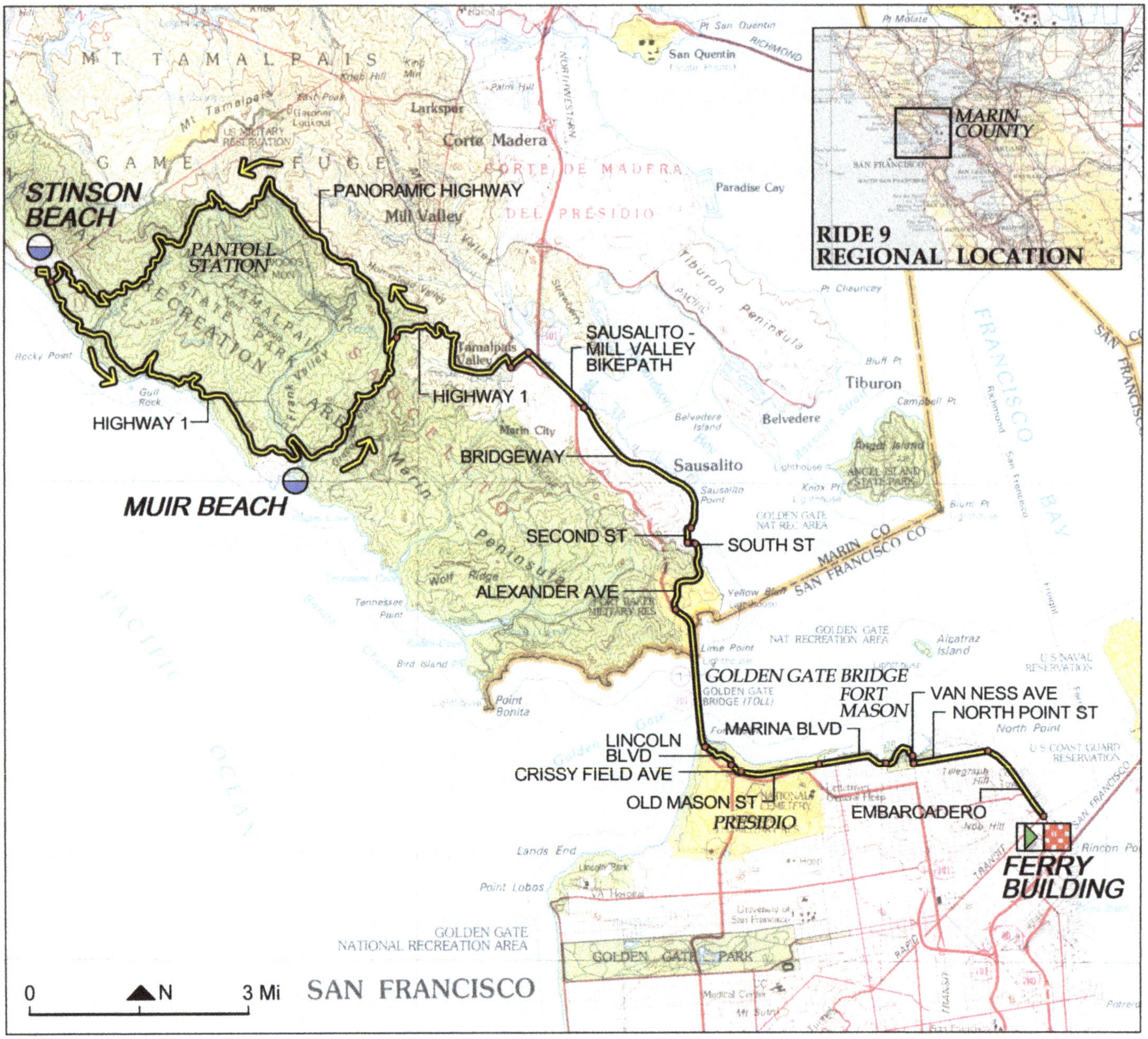

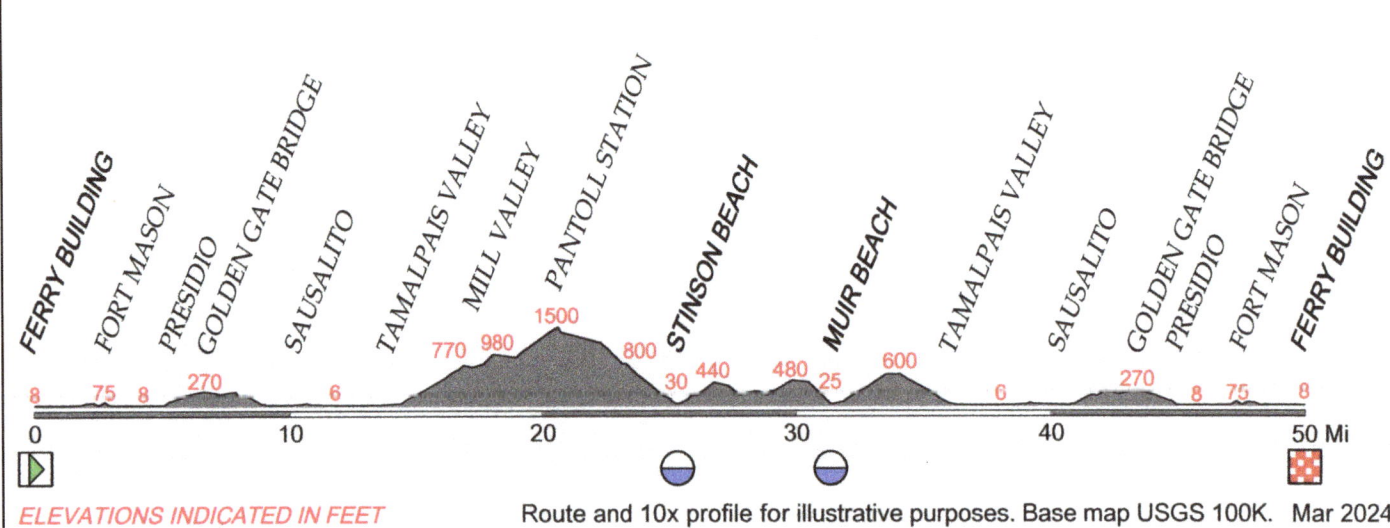

Ride 9: Stinson Beach/Muir Beach

This ride presents a middle distance climbing ride through the urban and adjacent parkland and mountain landscape of southern Marin County. Perhaps not as well-known as the 'signature' Mount Tamalpais climb is, this ride is arguably *more* challenging, with often windy conditions and enough climbing directly along the coast to reach a total of nearly 3900 feet. Repeated sustained efforts are required on the steeper climbing segments, and whether ridden as a recreational ride or as training, this one is tough — a fit rider will typically need three hours or more to complete the ride and return to San Francisco.

As with the Mount Tamalpais climb, some of the steeper sections provide opportunities to enjoy the very picturesque and beautiful views of the Bay and Pacific Ocean, southern Marin County, Stinson Beach, Bolinas and — under clear skies — the distant Point Reyes Peninsula. At roughly 50 miles, it is a medium distance ride, but nonetheless notable due to the spectacular setting and the steep climbing involved. Depending on the amount of auto traffic present, the descents can be speedy or slow, exhilarating or nerve wracking, but nonetheless remain a worthwhile part of the challenge. Serious cyclists training for longer events make this tough workout a regular part of their regimen.

The route begins at the San Francisco Ferry Building and proceeds north and west along the Bay into the Presidio of San Francisco before crossing the Golden Gate Bridge. Riders then descend into Sausalito and continue to Tamalpais Valley Junction, where the Highway 1 climb to the Panoramic Highway and Pantoll Station begins. From there, the route descends to the coast just south of Stinson Beach, first destination point of the ride.

The return south along Highway 1 begins with a steady, steep ascent along the coastal bluff followed by a steep, rapid descent into Muir Beach, the ride's second destination. After a final 600 foot climb and descent over Highway 1 to Tamalpais Valley Junction, the route continues to Sausalito along a 1.5 mile segment of flat bike path, follows the bay front through town and then climbs to the Golden Gate Bridge. After crossing southbound, riders continue through the Presidio and along the City's northern waterfront to Justin Herman Plaza, at the foot of Market Street. Depending on time of day, the Golden Gate Ferry may provide an alternative for return from Sausalito to the San Francisco Ferry Building.

Ride Characteristics

Difficulty: High

Distance: 50 miles

Terrain: Mixed flat and hilly, with short, steep climbing and descending sections within Fort Mason and the Presidio. Several sustained, moderate and steep climbing sections, the seven mile climb to Pantoll Station on Mount Tamalpais, a five and a half mile climb along the coastal headland from Stinson Beach to Muir Beach, and a three mile climb from Muir Beach to Tamalpais Valley Junction. Steady, steep descents from Pantoll Station to Stinson Beach, into Muir Beach, followed by the more gradual downhill into Tamalpais Valley Junction.

Elevation Range: Approximately 5 feet to 1500 feet above sea level.

Climbing: Approx. 3880 feet

Situation: Urban and urban parkland setting; Bridge walkway; rural segments of two lane highway.

Road Conditions: Street traffic and pedestrians, moderate to heavy; road surfaces, good to rough, slippery on foggy or overcast wet morning descents through wooded parklands.

Weather: Sea breezes off the bay and ocean can provide a substantial wind factor. Strong winds from the west can make crossing the Golden Gate Bridge challenging, especially while maneuvering around the towers. Morning conditions can often be cool and cloudy. Summer and Fall afternoon temperatures can be hot.

Notes: Bike shops numbered 1 through 7 and 24 through 27 in Appendix 1 are found in the general vicinity traversed along this route through San Francisco and Marin County. Nevertheless, shops are not always open or nearby — carrying essential tools, a pump, a tire repair kit and 2 tubes is highly recommended. This ride also includes significant segments of rural road where there are *no* services.

Approximate Ride Time: 3 to 4 hours.

Detailed Route Directions

Begin the ride in front of the Ferry Building and proceed north along the Embarcadero using the two-way, signed and green-painted bike lane. This lane is preferable for most cyclists, compared to the heavily-walked San Francisco Bay Trail segment located along the east sidewalk of the Embarcadero. The bike lane becomes one-way 'northbound' at Broadway. Continue in the bike lane to North Point Street. Use the signed and painted bike lane to cross the Embarcadero and turn left on to North Point Street. Ride along North Point Street, climbing steadily for two blocks at Columbus Avenue and continuing past Ghirardelli Square to Van Ness Avenue. Turn right on Van Ness Avenue and descend two blocks to its end, at the Aquatic Park Municipal Pier.

Turn left before the pier and ride into Fort Mason. The short climb up the former McDowell Avenue and around Black Point requires about five minutes of riding in a low gear or pedaling out of the saddle to gain about 65 feet of elevation. Watch for pedestrians and other cyclists walking bikes or those who stop along the San Francisco Bay Trail to view the Golden Gate Bridge. Other bicyclists may also stop suddenly on the steep incline after neglecting to shift into an easier gear. Still other cyclists may be descending rapidly from the opposite direction.

On a clear day, cyclists will enjoy stunning vistas of San Francisco Bay and the Golden Gate Bridge before descending past Fort Mason's Great Meadow to the pan-flat Marina Boulevard. This part of the route is just eight to ten feet above the bay's elevation. Proceed along Marina Boulevard past Gaslight Cove, the Marina Green and the St. Francis Yacht Club into the Presidio, where Marina Boulevard intersects Old Mason Street at Yacht Road.

Follow Old Mason Street through the Presidio adjacent to the restored wetlands and Crissy Field, turn left and then quickly right on Crissy Field Avenue and climb the short, steep pitch a few hundred feet to Lincoln Boulevard. Having gained about fifty feet of elevation, turn right at the stop sign and follow Lincoln Boulevard, past Long Avenue, climbing gradually to Battery East Road. Bear right on Battery East Road, which merges immediately with the Battery East Trail. Ride along the Battery East Trail and follow the signs indicating directions to approach the Golden Gate Bridge's east-side or west-side walkways.[18] Watch for westerly winds, southbound cyclists and pedestrians on the bridge.

---

[18] Detailed instructions for crossing the Golden Gate Bridge, northbound, are included on page 40.

Once across the bridge, continue north from either walkway to Alexander Avenue. Follow the winding Alexander Avenue through the rolling terrain of Fort Baker, and descend into the City of Sausalito where Alexander Avenue becomes South Street. Continue on South Street to Second Street. Turn right on Second Street and ride to Richardson Street. Bear right on to Richardson Street, which becomes Bridgeway one block to the east.

Downtown Sausalito is completely flat and often full of walking *and* cycling tourists. The geographic setting along the bay is undeniably inviting. The weather can be warm and sunny when San Francisco is breezy, gray and foggy. Use extra caution along Bridgeway — pedestrians may cross the street mid-block or against traffic signals. Continue north through the city past the marinas and waterfront restaurants, Dunphy Park, and the Marinship area to Gate Six Road, just west of the houseboat marinas at Waldo Point.

Cross Gate Six Road and enter the Sausalito-Mill Valley bike path. Continue north on the path about a mile to its intersection with the Coyote Creek bike path, which connects west to Tamalpais Valley Junction. Turn left and follow the flat path adjacent to Coyote Creek, less than a half-mile, to Highway 1 in Tamalpais Valley Junction. Turn right onto Highway 1 and continue another quarter-mile to reach its intersection with Almonte Boulevard.

Turn left at Almonte Boulevard to remain on Highway 1 and begin the ride's first serious climbing. Continue along Highway 1 steadily gaining about 700 feet of elevation before the road levels off near Panoramic Highway. Shift to a low gear and bear right on Panoramic Highway. Once beyond the first short rise remain in a very low gear and climb the steep, tight, hairpin turn that follows, quickly gaining about 20-30 feet of elevation in just a hundred feet of road distance. Ride along the next flatter section of Panoramic Highway to its intersection with Sequoia Valley Road and Muir Woods Road.[19]

Continue on Panoramic Highway past Sequoia Valley Road and Muir Woods Road, beginning the second steeper section, climbing to an elevation of about 1000 feet at Mountain Home Inn. Ride into Mount Tamalpais State Park and follow Panoramic Highway as it climbs another 500 feet to Pantoll Road.[20] Several switchback turns along the way require shifting to a low gear and/or pedaling while riding 'out of the saddle.'

Panoramic Highway reaches its crest at Pantoll Station. The adjacent parking area is a logical place for a brief stop to put on a jacket before continuing on Panoramic Highway. From there, begin a descent of several miles along a wooded, technical downhill section of the road parallel to Webb Creek. Once out of the woods continue with caution through five steep, switchback turns reaching an elevation of just 30 feet or so above sea level at Highway 1. Turn right on Highway 1 and ride north into the town of Stinson Beach.

Stinson Beach is the first destination point of the ride. The intersection of Highway 1 and Calle del Mar is a logical place for a rest stop. The Stinson Beach Market is directly up the hill and Village Green Park is situated across the Highway to the west.

After a look around town, it's a good time to check the tires and get back on the bike

---

[19] Also known as 'Four Corners.'
[20] Elevation 1500 feet.

Bolinas Lagoon and Mesa / Panoramic Highway

to begin the return to San Francisco. Ride south on Highway 1 and begin climbing, first past the intersection with Panoramic Highway, and then along the next steeply-inclined section of Highway 1 cut directly into the coastal bluff. Pass the Red Rock and Steep Ravine Trailheads as well as Rocky Point Road. Climb a thousand feet or so beyond the Rocky Point Trailhead to the first of two places where Highway 1 turns inland to cross a stream.

Just above Gull Rock, Highway 1 turns sharply inland from the coast, descending about half a mile, where it crosses Lone Tree Creek. Slow down on the descent and be sure to select a low gear *before* making the switchback turn at the stream crossing and beginning the short steep climb to the next southbound section of the highway along the coastal bluff.

Gull Rock, Bolinas Mesa and Point Reyes Headlands (center horizon) / Highway 1

Muir Beach, Gull Rock (San Francisco Peninsula on horizon) / Highway 1

Continue another half mile or so, and then follow Highway 1 inland once again. Slow down and gear down, this time crossing Cold Stream before beginning the climb back towards the coastline and past Slide Ranch, to the crest of the coastal bluff.

Use caution on the short fast descent into Muir Beach — the ride's second destination. Make the ninety degree right hand turn at the base of the descent and turn right again at Muir Woods Road in order to stay on the flat section of Highway 1. Pass the Pelican Inn at Pacific Way and begin the last major climb of the day, winding steadily up Green Gulch parallel to the Zen Center farm on the south. Continue up Highway 1 to its crest at Panoramic Highway and begin the descent towards Tamalpais Valley Junction.

Turn right at the intersection of Almonte Boulevard and Highway 1 and continue on Highway 1, less than a quarter-mile, to the Coyote Creek bike path. Bear right onto the path and ride east, about a half-mile, to the Mill Valley-Sausalito bike path. Turn right and ride south along the one-mile segment to Gate Six Road and Bridgeway, Sausalito's main street. Cross to the southbound bike lane on Bridgeway and continue through the city, climbing gradually past the Marinship area before descending into downtown Sausalito.

Continue on Bridgeway to begin the last leg of the day's ride, proceeding through Sausalito along the bay shoreline to Richardson Street. Bear right on to Richardson Street and climb one block to Second Street. Bear left on to Second Street and continue climbing several short blocks to South Street. Bear left on to South Street, ride one block and then climb the short, steep pitch where South Street becomes Alexander Avenue. Continue on Alexander Avenue climbing steadily past East Road and Danes Drive in Fort Baker.

Climb on Alexander Avenue to the east-side or west-side Golden Gate Bridge walkway.[21] Watch for westerly winds, northbound cyclists and pedestrians on the bridge. After crossing the bridge, follow the Battery East Trail to Lincoln Boulevard. Turn left on Lincoln

[21] Detailed instructions for crossing the Golden Gate Bridge, southbound, are included on pages 41.

Boulevard and ride to Crissy Field Avenue. Turn left on to Crissy Field Avenue and descend to Old Mason Street. Turn right and ride on Old Mason Street to Marina Boulevard.

Continue east on Marina Boulevard to Fort Mason. Climb along the San Francisco Bay Trail through upper Fort Mason, past the Great Meadow and around Black Point, before descending to Van Ness Avenue and the foot of the Aquatic Park Municipal Pier. Climb gradually two blocks on Van Ness Avenue to North Point Street. Turn left and continue along North Point Street to the Embarcadero. Turn right on the Embarcadero and proceed to finish the ride at Justin Herman Plaza, just west of the Ferry Building.

Opposite: Muir Beach / Highway 1

RIDE 10 : POINT REYES NATIONAL SEASHORE

ELEVATIONS INDICATED IN FEET

Route and 10x profile for illustrative purposes. Base map USGS 100K. Mar 2024

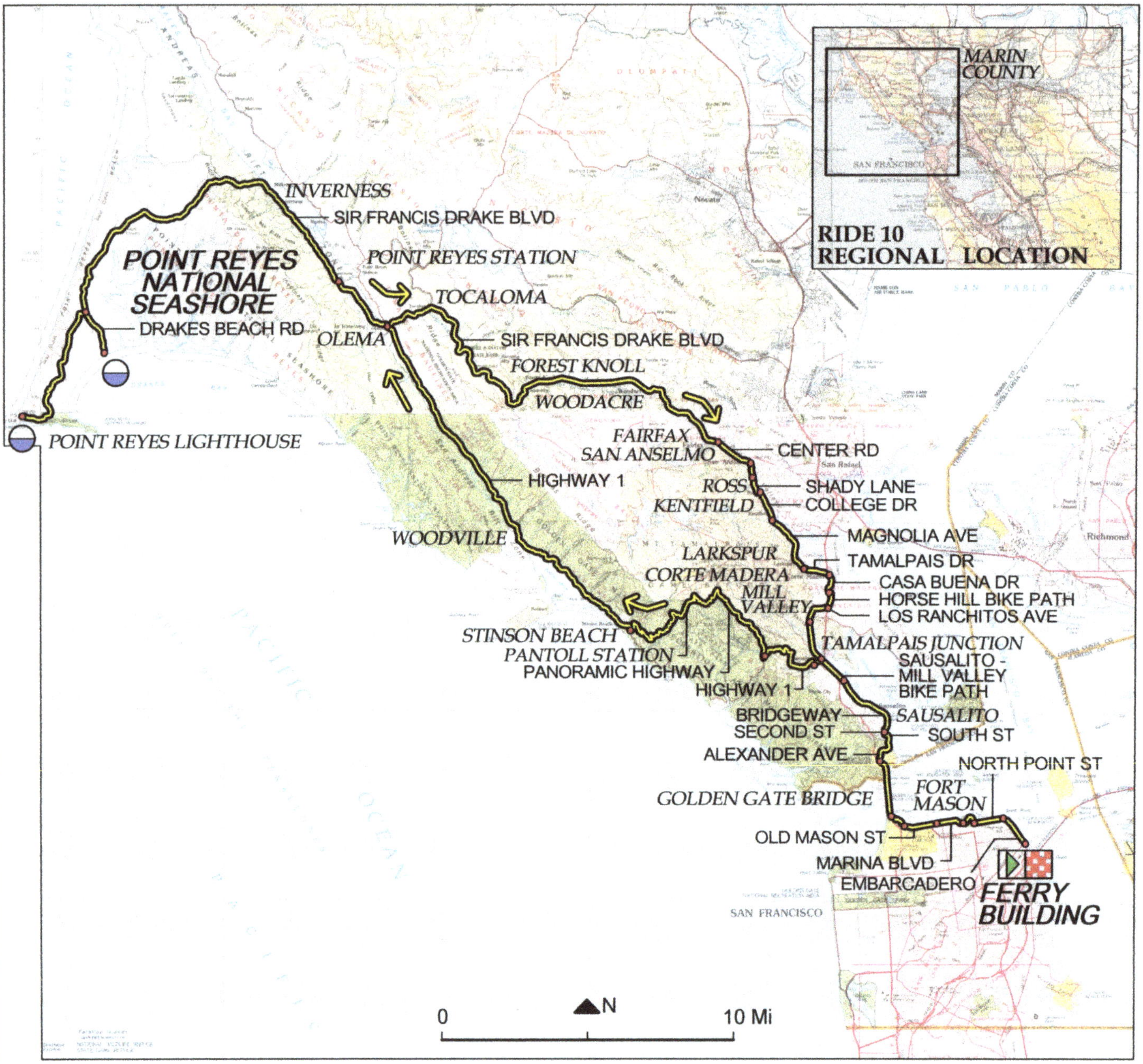

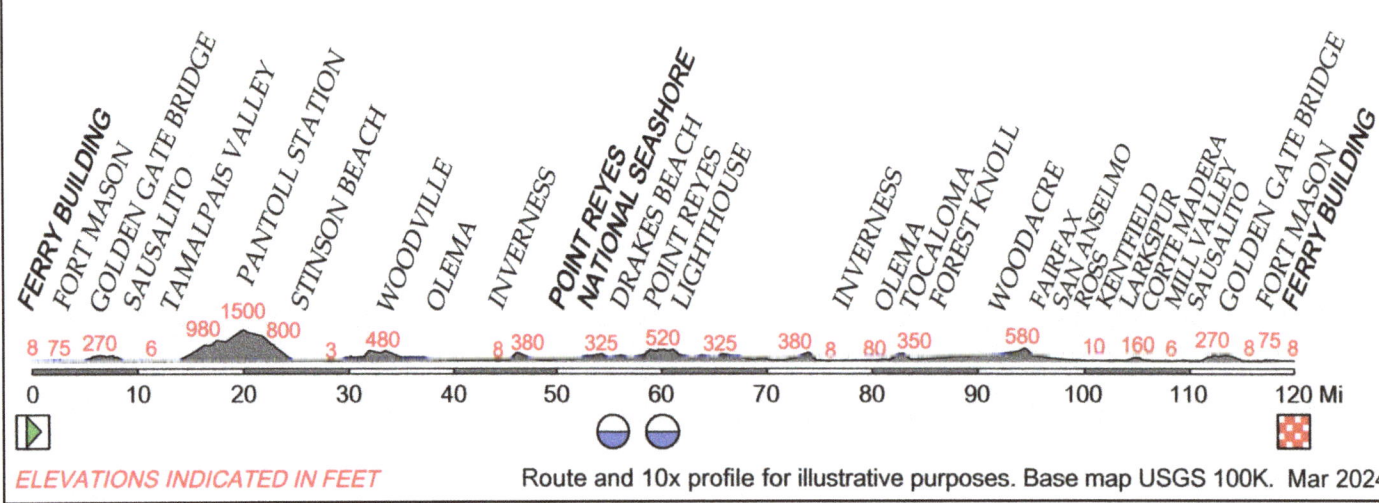

Ride 10: Point Reyes National Seashore

This ride presents perhaps the most ambitious route of all sixteen rides. It combines long distance with sustained climbing through the urban areas and adjacent mountain parklands of southern and west Marin County. The goal of reaching the lighthouse atop the Point Reyes headland is a serious challenge in any circumstances — one that many cyclists would never consider. It's an all-day affair with repeated efforts required on the numerous climbs. Ridden recreationally or as training, it takes about seven hours or more to complete the ride and return to San Francisco. Strong westerly winds can also make it a *long* day.

As with the other southern Marin County rides, the steep climbing and descent along Panoramic Highway provide opportunities to enjoy the picturesque scenery of southern Marin from along the ridgeline — Muir Woods, Stinson Beach, Bolinas, and the Point Reyes Peninsula are spectacular on a clear day. Highway 1 and Sir Francis Drake Boulevard pass seaside towns, oak woodlands, dairy lands and horse ranches. Beneath blue skies or even a thick layer of fog, views from the Point Reyes Lighthouse can also be stunning and unique.

At roughly 120 miles, the ride to Point Reyes is the longest of the sixteen rides — a major achievement due to the distance, spectacular setting and 6300 feet of climbing involved. Depending on the weather and amount of auto traffic, the technical descents can be speedy or slow, exhilarating or nerve wracking. This challenging, endurance ride is unforgettable.

The route begins at the San Francisco Ferry Building and proceeds north and west along the Bay into the Presidio of San Francisco before crossing the Golden Gate Bridge. Riders descend into Sausalito and continue to Tamalpais Valley Junction, where the Highway 1 climb to the Panoramic Highway and Pantoll Station begins. From there the route descends to the coast just south of Stinson Beach where cyclists ride along Highway One through Stinson Beach and past Woodville, to Olema and Inverness. After a steady ascent over Inverness ridge riders continue along Sir Francis Drake Boulevard to the Point Reyes Lighthouse atop the Point Reyes Headland or to Drakes Beach Road and Drakes Beach.[22]

The return follows Sir Francis Drake Boulevard to Inverness and Olema, then continues on Sir Francis Drake Boulevard past Samuel P. Taylor State Park and through the communities of Lagunitas, Forest Knolls, San Geronimo and Woodacre. A wide-shouldered bike lane continues over White Hill to Fairfax and quiet streets in San Anselmo, Ross and Kentfield traverse the flat lands leading south to Larkspur, Corte Madera and Mill Valley. A 2.5 mile segment of flat bike path reaches Sausalito, where riders follow the bay front through town and then climb to the Golden Gate Bridge. After crossing southbound, the route continues through the Presidio, and along the City's northern waterfront to Justin Herman Plaza, at the foot of Market Street. Depending on time of day, the Golden Gate Ferry may provide alternatives for return from Larkspur or Sausalito to the San Francisco Ferry Building.

---

[22] The segment of Sir Francis Drake Boulevard leading to the lighthouse, itself, is closed seasonally from December to March. Drakes Beach Road normally remains open during the winter months.

Ride Characteristics

Difficulty: High

Distance: 120 miles

Terrain: Mixed flat, rolling, and hilly, with short, steep climbing and descending sections in Fort Mason and the Presidio preceding the sustained, moderately steep, seven mile climb to Pantoll Station on Mount Tamalpais and a steep, four mile descent to Stinson Beach. Steady, steep climbing from Bolinas Lagoon to the rolling section of ranchland south of Olema; mostly flat along Tomales Bay to Inverness. Steady, steep climbing over Inverness Ridge, then flat and rolling before reaching the steep two mile climb leading to the Point Reyes Lighthouse. Steep descents from the lighthouse and Inverness Ridge on the return precede the more gradual climbs through Samuel P. Taylor State Park and from Lagunitas over White Hill to Fairfax.

Elevation Range: Approximately 3 feet to 1500 feet above sea level.

Climbing: Approx. 6300 feet

Situation: Urban and urban parkland setting; Bridge walkway; rural segments of two lane highway.

Road Conditions: Street traffic and pedestrians, moderate to heavy; road surfaces, good to rough, slippery on foggy or overcast wet morning descents through wooded parklands.

Weather: Sea breezes off the bay and ocean can provide a substantial wind factor. Strong winds from the west can make crossing the Golden Gate Bridge challenging, especially while maneuvering around the towers. Morning conditions can often be cool and cloudy. Summer and Fall afternoon temperatures can be hot.

Notes: Bike shops numbered 1 through 7 and 24 through 34 in Appendix 1 are found in the general vicinity traversed along this route through San Francisco and Marin County. Nevertheless, shops are not always open or nearby — carrying essential tools, a pump, a tire repair kit and 2 tubes is highly recommended. This ride also includes lengthy segments of park road and rural road where there are *no* services.

Approximate Ride Time: 6 to 7 hours.

Detailed Route Directions

Begin the ride in front of the Ferry Building and proceed north along the Embarcadero using the two-way, signed and green-painted bike lane. This lane is preferable for most cyclists, compared to the heavily-walked San Francisco Bay Trail segment located along the east sidewalk of the Embarcadero. The bike lane becomes one-way 'northbound' at Broadway. Continue in the bike lane to North Point Street. Use the signed and painted bike lane to cross the Embarcadero and turn left on to North Point Street. Ride along North Point Street, climbing steadily for two blocks at Columbus Avenue and continuing past Ghirardelli Square to Van Ness Avenue. Turn right on Van Ness Avenue and descend two blocks to its end, at the Aquatic Park Municipal Pier.

Turn left before the pier and ride into Fort Mason. The short climb up the former McDowell Avenue and around Black Point requires about five minutes of riding in a low gear or pedaling out of the saddle to gain about 65 feet of elevation. Watch for pedestrians and other cyclists walking bikes or those who stop along the San Francisco Bay Trail to view the Golden Gate Bridge. Other bicyclists may also stop suddenly on the steep incline after neglecting to shift into an easier gear. Still other cyclists may be descending rapidly from the opposite direction.

On a clear day, cyclists will enjoy stunning vistas of San Francisco Bay and the Golden Gate Bridge before descending past Fort Mason's Great Meadow to the pan-flat Marina Boulevard. This part of the route is just eight to ten feet above the bay's elevation. Proceed along Marina Boulevard past Gaslight Cove, the Marina Green and the St. Francis Yacht Club into the Presidio, where Marina Boulevard intersects Old Mason Street at Yacht Road.

Follow Old Mason Street through the Presidio adjacent to the restored wetlands and Crissy Field, turn left and then quickly right on Crissy Field Avenue and climb the short, steep pitch a few hundred feet to Lincoln Boulevard. Having gained about fifty feet of elevation, turn right at the stop sign and follow Lincoln Boulevard, past Long Avenue, climbing gradually to Battery East Road. Bear right on Battery East Road, which merges immediately with the Battery East Trail. Ride along the Battery East Trail and follow the signs indicating directions to approach the Golden Gate Bridge's east-side or west-side walkways.[23] Watch for westerly winds, southbound cyclists and pedestrians on the bridge.

Once across the bridge, continue north from either walkway to Alexander Avenue. Follow the winding Alexander Avenue through the rolling terrain of Fort Baker, and descend into the City of Sausalito where Alexander Avenue becomes South Street. Continue on South Street to Second Street. Turn right on to Second Street and ride to Richardson Street. Bear right on to Richardson Street, which becomes Bridgeway one block to the east.

Downtown Sausalito is completely flat and often full of walking *and* cycling tourists. The geographic setting along the bay is undeniably inviting. The weather can be warm and sunny when San Francisco is breezy, gray and foggy. Use extra caution along Bridgeway — pedestrians may cross the street mid-block or against traffic signals. Continue north through the city past the marinas and waterfront restaurants, Dunphy Park, and the Marinship area to Gate Six Road, just west of the houseboat marinas at Waldo Point.

Cross Gate Six Road and enter the Sausalito-Mill Valley bike path. Continue north on the path about a mile to its intersection with the Coyote Creek bike path, which connects west to Tamalpais Valley Junction. Turn left and follow the flat path adjacent to Coyote Creek, less than a half-mile, to Highway 1 in Tamalpais Valley Junction. Turn right onto Highway 1 and continue another quarter-mile to reach its intersection with Almonte Boulevard.

Turn left at Almonte Boulevard to remain on Highway 1 and begin the ride's first serious climbing. Continue along Highway 1 steadily gaining about 700 feet of elevation before the road levels off near Panoramic Highway. Shift to a low gear and bear right on Panoramic Highway. Once beyond the first short rise remain in a very low gear and climb the steep, tight, hairpin turn that follows, quickly gaining about 20-30 feet of elevation in just a hundred feet of road distance. Ride along the next flatter section of Panoramic Highway to its intersection with Sequoia Valley Road and Muir Woods Road.[24]

Continue on Panoramic Highway past Sequoia Valley Road and Muir Woods Road, beginning the second steeper section, climbing to an elevation of about 1000 feet at Mountain Home Inn. Ride into Mount Tamalpais State Park and follow Panoramic Highway as it

---

[23] Detailed instructions for crossing the Golden Gate Bridge, northbound, are included on page 40.
[24] Also known as 'Four Corners.'

climbs another 500 feet to Pantoll Road.[25] Several switchback turns along the way require shifting to a low gear and/or pedaling while riding 'out of the saddle.'

Panoramic Highway reaches its crest at Pantoll Station. The adjacent parking area is a logical place for a brief stop to put on a jacket before continuing on Panoramic Highway. From there, begin a descent of several miles along a wooded, technical downhill section of the road parallel to Webb Creek. Once out of the woods continue with caution through five steep, switchback turns reaching an elevation of just 30 feet or so above sea level at Highway 1. Turn right on Highway 1 and ride north into the town of Stinson Beach.

Stinson Beach is considered the first logical rest stop for this ride. Whether or not a stop was made at Pantoll Station, the intersection of Highway 1 and Calle del Mar in central Stinson Beach is a convenient place to stretch, rehydrate and eat something. The Stinson Beach Market is directly up the hill and a small park is situated across the Highway to the west. A stop here also presents an opportunity to check the tires before continuing north. More than three quarters of the ride distance remains and there is still substantial climbing ahead — any possibility of a flat tire somewhere should be minimized.

Begin the next leg of the journey on Highway 1 riding immediately along the shoreline of Bolinas Lagoon. Pass the turn to Bolinas-Fairfax Road and begin the steeper 500 foot climb through the woodland north of Bolinas Lagoon to Woodville, where Highway 1 flattens out a bit. Continue through the rolling terrain and past several large horse ranches before reaching the town of Olema. Follow Highway 1, past the Druids Hall and the Olema Farmhouse, to Bear Valley Road. Turn left on Bear Valley Road and ride past the Point Reyes National Seashore Visitor Center, to Sir Francis Drake Boulevard.

Bear left on to Sir Francis Drake Boulevard and continue through Inverness Park and into the town of Inverness on the southwest shore of Tomales Bay. Remain on Sir Francis Drake Boulevard as it heads out of town and turns west, presenting the first climbing on the Point Reyes Peninsula itself. Once inside the Point Reyes National Seashore, continue on Sir Francis Drake Boulevard through the rolling terrain, past Pierce Point Road and the Drakes Bay oyster farm road, to Drakes Beach Road. From December through March continue the ride on Drakes Beach Road, descending two miles to the Drakes Beach parking lot — wintertime destination and turnaround point of the ride.

From April through November the preferred option is to continue riding south on Sir Francis Drake Boulevard another rolling 6.5 miles or so to the Point Reyes Lighthouse, itself. After reaching the southern end of the Great Beach, climb the headland along the final few steep miles, gaining about 500 feet of elevation before arriving at the Lighthouse Visitor Center — destination and turnaround point of the ride.

The return directions to Inverness are simple: follow Sir Francis Drake Boulevard. Once in Inverness, continue through town on Sir Francis Drake Boulevard and past Inverness Park to Bear Valley Road. Turn right on Bear Valley Road and continue to Olema.

Bear Valley Road ends at Highway 1 in Olema. Turn right on Highway 1 and ride south just 600 feet to Sir Francis Drake Boulevard. Turn left on Sir Francis Drake Boulevard and begin a long, gradual climb alongside Lagunitas Creek, past Samuel P. Taylor State Park, and through the San Geronimo Valley communities of Lagunitas, Forest Knolls, San Geronimo and Woodacre. Begin the last climb on Sir Francis Drake Boulevard — over White Hill.

[25] Elevation 1500 feet.

Opposite Page: Point Reyes Lighthouse (u) and Great Beach (l)

The crest of White Hill is at an elevation of just 600 feet or so, but it separates the San Geronimo Valley communities, at an elevation of 300 feet or so, from the towns of Fairfax, San Anselmo, Ross, and Kentfield, all situated mostly at or below 50 feet elevation and closer to the bay shoreline. As a result, the climb is a gradual incline from Woodacre over White Hill followed by a speedy downhill to Fairfax.

Begin the climb in a low gear and ride steadily to the crest of White Hill. The descent can be a speedy one if road conditions and traffic allow. Once in Fairfax slow down and continue on Sir Francis Drake Boulevard to Claus Drive. Turn left on Claus Drive to visit the Marin Museum of Bicycling,[26] otherwise turn right on Claus Drive and ride one block to Broadway Boulevard. Turn left on Broadway Boulevard and continue to Pacheco Avenue, where the Broadway Boulevard becomes Center Boulevard in San Anselmo.

Ride along Center Boulevard to Grove Lane. Turn right on Grove Lane then turn left immediately on San Anselmo Avenue. Continue on San Anselmo Avenue through the commercial district and southerly to Bolinas Avenue. Turn right on Bolinas Avenue and proceed one block to Shady Lane. Turn left on Shady Lane and ride to Lagunitas Road. Turn left on Lagunitas Road and ride one block to Ross Common. Turn right on Ross Common and proceed south where the street name changes from Poplar Avenue to Kent Avenue, in the community of Kentfield.

Continue on Kent Avenue to its intersection with College Avenue. Bear right on to College Avenue, which becomes Magnolia Avenue in the City of Larkspur. Continue along Magnolia Avenue through the commercial section of Larkspur, and eventually to Tamalpais Drive and Redwood Avenue in Corte Madera. Turn left on Tamalpais Drive, ride downhill through two short, sweeping turns to the flat section of Tamalpais Drive and ride directly through Corte Madera east toward Highway 101.

Continue on Tamalpais Avenue to Sanford Street and Madera Boulevard. Turn right on Sanford Street and then left on Meadowsweet Drive. Turn left on Meadowsweet Drive, ride past the Corte Madera Library, and climb gradually to the Horse Hill bike path, adjacent to Highway 101. Turn right and ride along the bike path to Lomita Drive.

Exit the Horse Hill bike path on Lomita Drive and proceed on Lomita Drive two blocks to Shell Road. Turn left on Shell Road and descend quickly one block to Meadow Drive. Turn left on Meadow Drive and again descend one block to Tower Drive. Turn left on Tower Drive and continue to East Blithedale Avenue.

Turn right on East Blithedale Avenue and proceed to Ashford Avenue. Bear right on Ashford Avenue, just before the Chevron Station, and continue four blocks to Lomita Drive. Turn left on Lomita Drive and ride to East Blithedale Avenue.

Cross East Blithedale Avenue to enter the Mill Valley-Sausalito bike path. Ride south along the flat 2.5 mile path to Gate Six Road and Bridgeway, Sausalito's main street. Cross to the southbound bike lane on Bridgeway and continue through the city, climbing gradually past the Marinship area before descending into downtown Sausalito.

Continue on Bridgeway to begin the last leg of the day's ride, proceeding through Sausalito along the bay shoreline to Richardson Street. Bear right on to Richardson Street and climb one block to Second Street. Bear left on to Second Street and continue climbing

---

[26] The Museum displays bicycles from the 19th century through the present day and showcases the birth and evolution of the mountain bike.

several short blocks to South Street. Bear left on to South Street, ride one block and then climb the short, steep pitch where South Street becomes Alexander Avenue. Continue on Alexander Avenue climbing steadily past East Road and Danes Drive in Fort Baker.

Climb on Alexander Avenue to the east-side or west-side Golden Gate Bridge walkway.[27] Watch for westerly winds, northbound cyclists and pedestrians on the bridge. After crossing the bridge, follow the Battery East Trail to Lincoln Boulevard. Turn left on Lincoln Boulevard and ride to Crissy Field Avenue. Turn left on to Crissy Field Avenue and descend to Old Mason Street. Turn right and ride on Old Mason Street to Marina Boulevard.

Continue east on Marina Boulevard to Fort Mason. Climb along the San Francisco Bay Trail through upper Fort Mason, past the Great Meadow and around Black Point, before descending to Van Ness Avenue and the foot of the Aquatic Park Municipal Pier. Climb gradually two blocks on Van Ness Avenue to North Point Street. Turn left and continue along North Point Street to the Embarcadero. Turn right on the Embarcadero and proceed to finish the ride at Justin Herman Plaza, just west of the Ferry Building.

---

[27] Detailed instructions for crossing the Golden Gate Bridge, southbound, are included on page 41.

RIDE 11 : MARIN FRENCH CHEESE COMPANY

ELEVATIONS INDICATED IN FEET

Route and 10x profile for illustrative purposes. Base map USGS 100K. Mar 2024

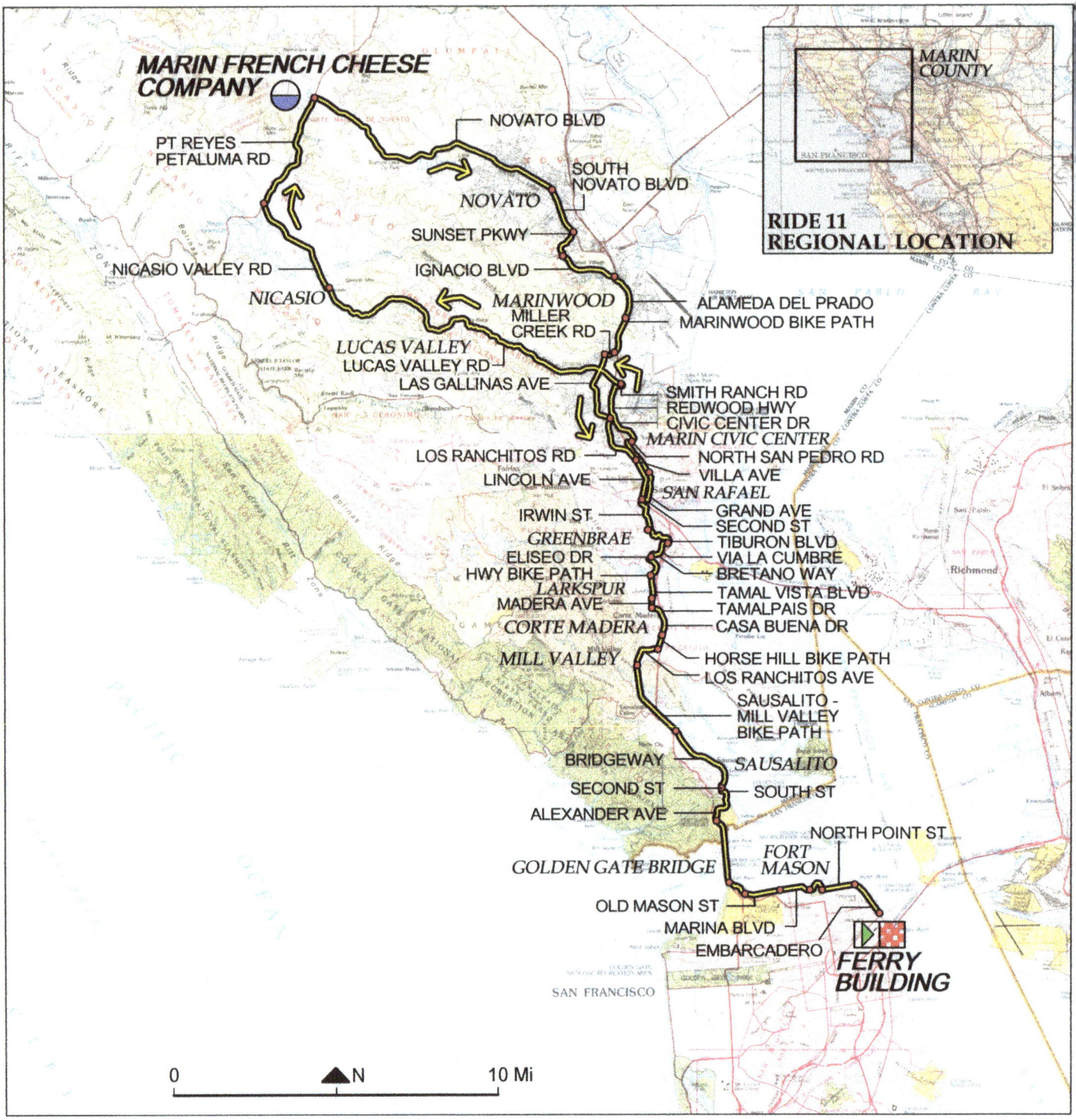

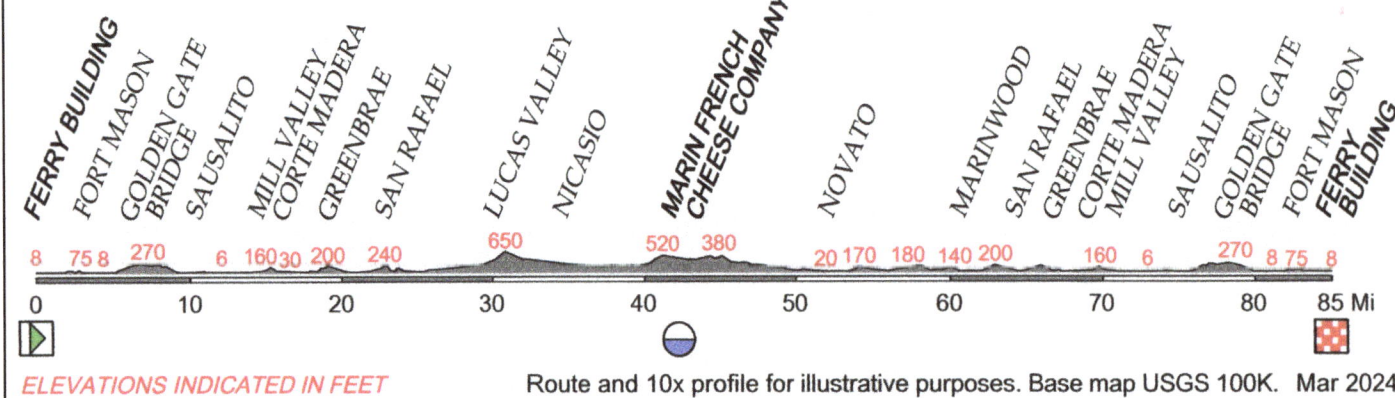

Ride 11: Marin French Cheese Company[28]

This ride presents another opportunity for cyclists interested in great scenery *and* endurance. The 'Cheese Factory' is a favorite destination for a longer, flatter jaunt from San Francisco. Also an achievement in suburban navigation, finishing the ride can leave cyclists feeling as though they've ridden, perhaps using the shortest possible route, to a place that *seems* much farther away from the start than it *really* is — one they might have returned from in just a few hours! — The route combines suburban riding with tranquil vistas along scenic valley roads — a rolling 85-mile distance with 3800 feet of climbing, through the urban communities, adjacent woodlands and watershed lands of beautiful West Marin County.

The Cheese Factory ride is *fun* — perhaps less strenuous than some of the other Marin rides — but still a fitness builder. Repeated sustained efforts are required on the brief, mildly steep climbs, stiff headwinds can be encountered and it can be very hot. Whether ridden recreationally or as training, this ride typically takes a fit rider four hours or so to complete. Along the way there are plenty of opportunities to enjoy views of the beautiful oak woodlands, reservoirs and pastoral valleys, west of Marinwood and Novato. Cycling along the flat and rolling rural roads is pleasant and relaxed.

The route begins just west of the Ferry Building and proceeds along the Bay waterfront to the Golden Gate Bridge, then across the bridge before descending into Sausalito, continuing through Mill Valley, Corte Madera, and Greenbrae to San Rafael. Once past the Marin County Civic Center riders continue through Terra Linda and then along Lucas Valley Road, climbing past Big Rock and descending to the Nicasio Valley. After riding through town and past Nicasio Reservoir, a steady climb of several miles along Point Reyes Petaluma Road eventually reaches the venerable and esteemed Marin French Cheese Company.

The return follows Novato Boulevard past Stafford Lake into the City of Novato, then parallels Highway 101 through Marin County's bayside communities of San Rafael, Greenbrae, Larkspur, Corte Madera, and Mill Valley. The mostly flat and rolling course includes some climbing and a 2.5 mile segment of flat bike path before reaching Sausalito, where riders follow the bay front through town and then climb to the Golden Gate Bridge. After crossing southbound, the route continues through the Presidio, and along the City's northern waterfront to Justin Herman Plaza, at the foot of Market Street. Depending on time of day, the Golden Gate Ferry may provide alternatives for return from Larkspur or Sausalito to the Ferry Building in San Francisco.

Ride Characteristics

Difficulty: Moderate
Distance: 85 miles
Terrain: Mixed flat and rolling, with several moderate and steep climbs and descents. Begins with short, steep climbing and descending sections in Fort Mason and the Presidio followed by flat and moderate to steep, short climbs between Mill Valley, Greenbrae and San Rafael. More sustained steeper climbs, first to Big Rock on Lucas Valley

---

[28] In operation since 1865 and considered the oldest, continuous cheese manufacturer in the United States.

Road and later along Pt. Reyes-Petaluma Road to the Marin French Cheese Company. Steady, sustained descents from Big Rock through Lucas Valley. Includes a final, moderate climbing section between San Rafael and Greenbrae along the return.

Elevation Range: Approximately sea level to 650 feet above sea level.

Climbing: Approx. 3830 feet

Situation: Urban and urban parkland setting; Bridge walkway; rural segments of two-lane highway.

Road Conditions: Street traffic and pedestrians, moderate to heavy; road surfaces, good to rough, slippery on foggy or overcast wet morning descents through wooded parklands.

Weather: Sea breezes off the bay and ocean can provide a substantial wind factor. Strong winds from the west can make crossing the Golden Gate Bridge challenging, especially while maneuvering around the towers. Morning conditions can often be cool and cloudy. Summer and Fall afternoon temperatures can be hot.

Notes: Bike shops numbered 1 through 7 and 24 through 35 in Appendix 1 are found in the general vicinity traversed along this route through San Francisco and Marin County. Nevertheless, shops are not always open or nearby — carrying essential tools, a pump, a tire repair kit and 2 tubes is highly recommended. This ride also includes significant segments of rural road where there are *no* services.

Approximate Ride Time: 4 to 5 hours.

Lucas Valley Road

Detailed Route Directions

Begin the ride in front of the Ferry Building and proceed north along the Embarcadero using the two-way, signed and green-painted bike lane. This lane is preferable for most cyclists, compared to the heavily-walked San Francisco Bay Trail segment located along the east sidewalk of the Embarcadero. The bike lane becomes one-way 'northbound' at Broadway. Continue in the bike lane to North Point Street. Use the signed and painted bike lane to cross the Embarcadero and turn left on to North Point Street. Ride along North Point Street, climbing steadily for two blocks at Columbus Avenue and continuing past Ghirardelli Square to Van Ness Avenue. Turn right on Van Ness Avenue and descend two blocks to its end, at the Aquatic Park Municipal Pier.

Turn left before the pier and ride into Fort Mason. The short climb up the former McDowell Avenue and around Black Point requires about five minutes of riding in a low gear or pedaling out of the saddle to gain about 65 feet of elevation. Watch for pedestrians and other cyclists walking bikes or those who stop along the San Francisco Bay Trail to view the Golden Gate Bridge. Other bicyclists may also stop suddenly on the steep incline after neglecting to shift into an easier gear. Still other cyclists may be descending rapidly from the opposite direction.

On a clear day, cyclists will enjoy stunning vistas of San Francisco Bay and the Golden Gate Bridge before descending past Fort Mason's Great Meadow to the pan-flat Marina Boulevard. This part of the route is just eight to ten feet above the bay's elevation. Proceed along Marina Boulevard past Gaslight Cove, the Marina Green and the St. Francis Yacht Club into the Presidio, where Marina Boulevard intersects Old Mason Street at Yacht Road.

Follow Old Mason Street through the Presidio adjacent to the restored wetlands and Crissy Field, turn left and then quickly right on Crissy Field Avenue and climb the short, steep pitch a few hundred feet to Lincoln Boulevard. Having gained about fifty feet of elevation, turn right at the stop sign and follow Lincoln Boulevard, past Long Avenue, climbing gradually to Battery East Road. Bear right on Battery East Road, which merges immediately with the Battery East Trail. Ride along the Battery East Trail and follow the signs indicating directions to approach the Golden Gate Bridge's east-side or west-side walkways.[29] Watch for westerly winds, southbound cyclists and pedestrians on the bridge.

Once across the bridge, continue north from either walkway to Alexander Avenue. Follow the winding Alexander Avenue through the rolling terrain of Fort Baker, and descend into the City of Sausalito where Alexander Avenue becomes South Street. Continue on South Street to Second Street. Turn right on Second Street and ride to Richardson Street. Bear right on to Richardson Street, which becomes Bridgeway one block to the east.

Downtown Sausalito is completely flat and often full of walking *and* cycling tourists. The geographic setting along the bay is undeniably inviting. The weather can be warm and sunny when San Francisco is breezy, gray and foggy. Use extra caution along Bridgeway — pedestrians may cross the street mid-block or against traffic signals. Continue north through the city past the marinas and waterfront restaurants, Dunphy Park, and the Marinship area to Gate Six Road, just west of the houseboat marinas at Waldo Point.

Cross Gate Six Road and enter the Sausalito-Mill Valley bike path. Continue north on

---

[29] Detailed instructions for crossing the Golden Gate Bridge, northbound, are included on pages 40.

Marin French Cheese Company / Pond and Picnic Area

Marin French Cheese Company

the flat 2.5 mile path, under the Richardson Bay Bridge, past Coyote Creek and the Bothin Marsh Preserve, to East Blithedale Avenue.

Cross East Blithedale Avenue and bear right on Lomita Drive. Continue on Lomita Drive which turns abruptly at the Edna Maguire Elementary School. Follow Lomita Drive and gradually climb to the short segment of paved bike path that continues over 'Horse Hill.' Ride along the path, climbing gradually to Casa Buena Drive.

Continue along Casa Buena Drive, past Marin Joe's Restaurant, to Sanford Street. Turn right on Sanford Street, cross Tamalpais Drive and continue on Madera Boulevard, past the Corte Madera Town Center mall to Tamal Vista Boulevard.

Bear left on Tamal Vista Boulevard and continue to Fifer Avenue. Turn left on Fifer Avenue and ride one block to Lucky Drive. Turn right on Lucky Drive and continue one and a half blocks to the bike path following the highway overcrossing at Corte Madera Creek.

The bike path at Corte Madera Creek is adjacent to Highway 101 — part of a low concrete bridge over the creek mouth, A short rise is followed by a quick descent to Sir Francis Drake Boulevard. Once north of the creek, continue on the Sir Francis Drake Boulevard bike path, one block to Eliseo Drive.

Cross Sir Francis Drake Boulevard at Eliseo Drive and begin the climb through Greenbrae, continuing on Eliseo Drive, past Bretano Way, to Via Hermosa. Turn right on Via Hermosa and ride to Via La Cumbre. Turn left on Via La Cumbre and ride along this flatter section of road, perched just west of Highway 101.

Continue on Via La Cumbre to Tiburon Boulevard. Bear right on Tiburon Boulevard and begin the descent from Greenbrae into San Rafael. Continue on Tiburon Boulevard to Irwin Street. Bear left on to Irwin Street and continue descending sinuously past Bret Harte Park to Lincoln Avenue, two blocks north of Anderson Drive.

Turn left on Lincoln Avenue and ride across San Rafael Creek to Fourth Street. Turn right on Fourth Street and ride through the Highway 101 underpass to Irwin Street. Turn left on Irwin Street and ride to Belle Avenue. Turn left on Belle Avenue and ride to Grand Avenue. Turn left on Grand Avenue and ride to its merges with Villa Avenue. Continue on Villa Avenue, past Lillian Lane, to the northbound on-ramp for Highway 101.

Proceed north onto Highway 101 and ride briefly along the highway shoulder bike lane — about half a mile — to North San Pedro Road. Bear right on to the North San Pedro Road off-ramp and continue to San Pablo Avenue and Civic Center Drive. Turn left on Civic Center Drive and ride to Manual T. Freitas Parkway and Old Redwood Highway. Cross Manual T. Freitas Parkway and continue on Old Redwood Highway to Smith Ranch Road. Turn left on Smith Ranch Road and ride towards Highway 101 where Smith Ranch Road becomes Lucas Valley Road and continues into Marinwood.

Proceed west on Lucas Valley Road and begin the climb to the crest — a point known as Big Rock. Continue on Lucas Valley Road, gradually descending adjacent to Nicasio Creek, past the Skywalker Ranch, to Nicasio Valley Road. Turn right on Nicasio Valley Road and ride into the town of Nicasio, making ninety degree left and right turns as you pass through the center of this small hamlet.

Nicasio / Saint Mary's Church

Nicasio Valley Road

Continue on Nicasio Valley Road riding out of town, past the school and adjacent to the eastern shore of Nicasio Reservoir, to Point Reyes-Petaluma Road. Turn right on Point Reyes-Petaluma Road and climb steeply, then steadily to the reach the Marin French Cheese Company — rest stop and destination point of the ride.

Begin the return trip by continuing on Point Reyes-Petaluma Road to the nearby intersection with Novato Boulevard. Turn right on Novato Boulevard and ride past Stafford Lake and into the City of Novato. Continue on Novato Boulevard through town to South Novato Boulevard. Turn right and follow South Novato Boulevard to Sunset Parkway. Turn right on Sunset Parkway and climb gradually to Ignacio Boulevard.

Turn left on Ignacio Boulevard and ride to Alameda del Prado. Turn right on Alameda del Prado and ride to Nave Drive. Just after crossing Nave Drive enter the Ponti Ridge bike path and ride adjacent to Highway 101.

Climb steadily along the paved trail and then descend into Marinwood, where the path intersects Miller Creek Road. Turn right on Miller Creek Road and ride just a few hundred feet to Las Gallinas Avenue. Turn left on Las Gallinas Avenue and ride to Manual T. Freitas Parkway. Cross Manual T. Freitas Parkway and continue on Las Gallinas Avenue several blocks, where it becomes Los Ranchitos Road.

Continue south on Los Ranchitos Road and climb gradually towards Highway 101, where Los Ranchitos Road becomes Lincoln Avenue. Climb over the crest on Lincoln Avenue just west of Highway 101 and then descend quickly into downtown San Rafael. Continue on Lincoln Avenue, cross San Rafael Creek and continue to Irwin Street. Bear right on Irwin Street and ride south, crossing Anderson Avenue and Woodland Avenue before reaching Bret Harte Park and beginning the steady climb towards Greenbrae.

Climb Irwin Street to Tiburon Boulevard, and then continue climbing Tiburon Boulevard to Via La Cumbre. Bear right on to Via La Cumbre and ride to Via Hermosa. Bear right on Via Hermosa and immediately left on Bretano Way. Descend quickly along Bretano Way, one block to Eliseo Drive. Turn left on Eliseo Drive and ride to Sir Francis Drake Boulevard.

Cross to the south side of Sir Francis Drake Boulevard, and immediately turn left, entering the bike lane and riding towards Highway 101. Climb in the separated bike path adjacent to the on-ramp to Highway 101 overcrossing at Corte Madera Creek. After descending from the short bridge, follow the bike path to Lucky Drive. Continue on Lucky Drive two blocks to Fifer Avenue. Turn left on to Fifer Avenue and ride one block to Tamal Vista Boulevard.

From this point the ride follows the earlier northbound directions in their reverse order. Continue on Tamal Vista Boulevard to Madera Boulevard. Bear right on Madera Boulevard and ride past the Corte Madera Town Center mall to Tamalpais Drive. Cross Tamalpais Drive and continue on Sanford Street to Meadowsweet Drive. Turn left on Meadowsweet Drive, ride past the Corte Madera Library and climb gradually to the Horse Hill bike path west of Highway 101. Turn right and ride along the bike path to Lomita Drive.

Exit the Horse Hill bike path and proceed on Lomita Drive two blocks to Shell Road. Turn left on Shell Road and descend quickly one block to Meadow Drive. Turn left on to Meadow Drive and again descend one block to Tower Drive. Turn left on Tower Drive and continue to East Blithedale Avenue.

Turn right on East Blithedale Avenue and proceed to Ashford Avenue. Bear right on to Ashford Avenue, just before the Chevron Station and continue four blocks to Lomita Drive. Turn left on Lomita Drive and ride to East Blithedale Avenue.

Cross East Blithedale Avenue to enter the Mill Valley-Sausalito bike path. Ride south along the flat 2.5 mile path to Gate Six Road and Bridgeway, Sausalito's main street. Cross to the southbound bike lane on Bridgeway and continue through the city, climbing gradually past the Marinship area before descending into downtown Sausalito.

Continue on Bridgeway to begin the last leg of the day's ride, proceeding through Sausalito along the bay shoreline to Richardson Street. Bear right on to Richardson Street and climb one block to Second Street. Bear left on to Second Street and continue climbing several short blocks to South Street. Bear left on to South Street, ride one block and then climb the short, steep pitch where South Street becomes Alexander Avenue. Continue on Alexander Avenue climbing steadily past East Road and Danes Drive in Fort Baker.

Climb on Alexander Avenue to the east-side or west-side Golden Gate Bridge walkway.[30] Watch for westerly winds, northbound cyclists and pedestrians on the bridge. After crossing the bridge, follow the Battery East Trail to Lincoln Boulevard. Turn left on Lincoln Boulevard and ride to Crissy Field Avenue. Turn left on to Crissy Field Avenue and descend to Old Mason Street. Turn right and ride on Old Mason Street to Marina Boulevard.

Continue east on Marina Boulevard to Fort Mason. Climb along the San Francisco Bay Trail through upper Fort Mason, past the Great Meadow and around Black Point, before descending to Van Ness Avenue and the foot of the Aquatic Park Municipal Pier. Climb gradually two blocks on Van Ness Avenue to North Point Street. Turn left and continue along North Point Street to the Embarcadero. Turn right on the Embarcadero and proceed to finish the ride at Justin Herman Plaza, just west of the Ferry Building..

---

[30] Detailed instructions for crossing the Golden Gate Bridge, southbound, are included on page 41.

Opposite: Climbing Point Reyes-Petaluma Road

RIDE 12 : THE THREE BEARS / BRIONES VALLEY

ELEVATIONS INDICATED IN FEET

Route and 10x profile for illustrative purposes. Base map USGS 100K. Mar 2024

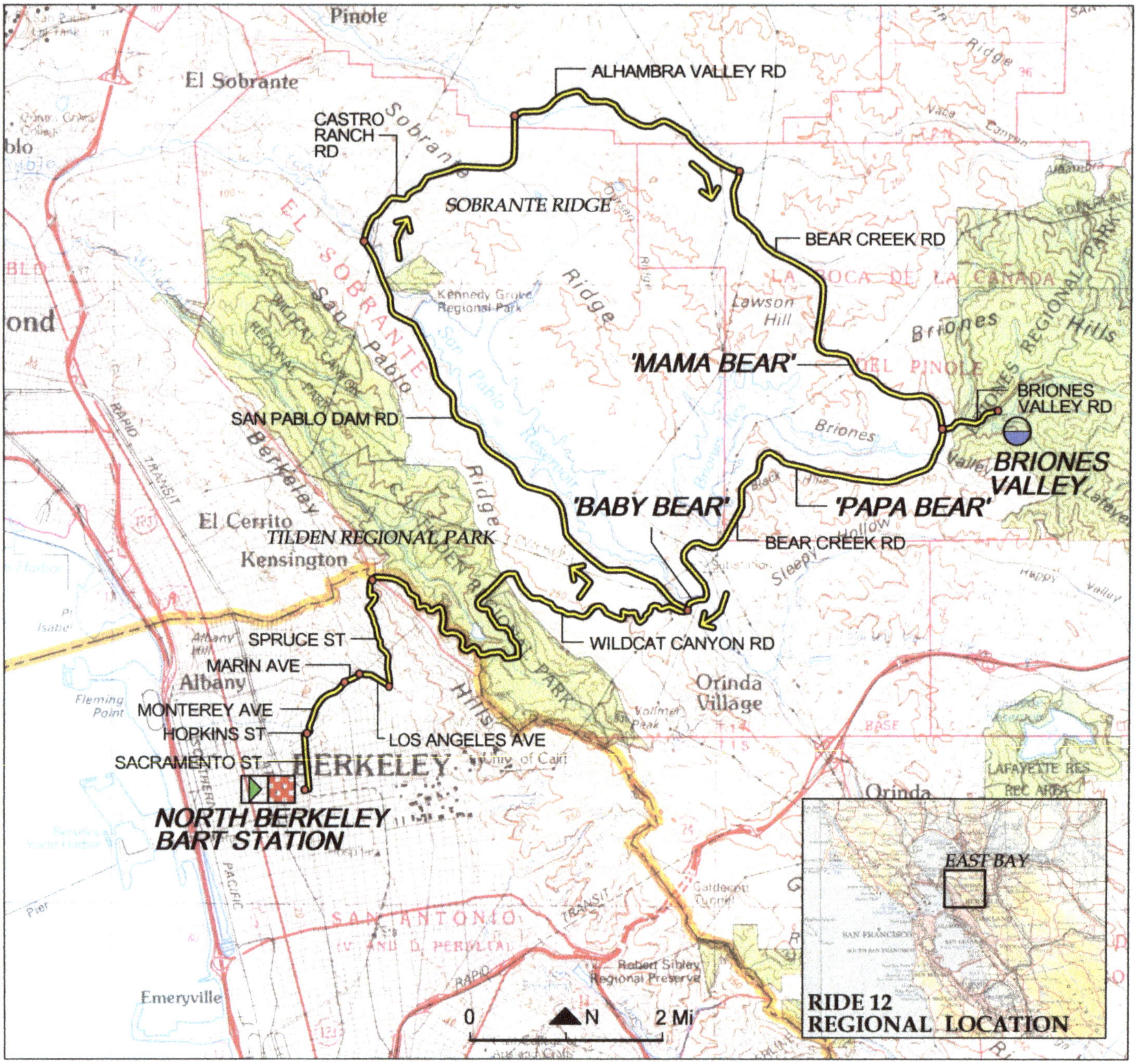

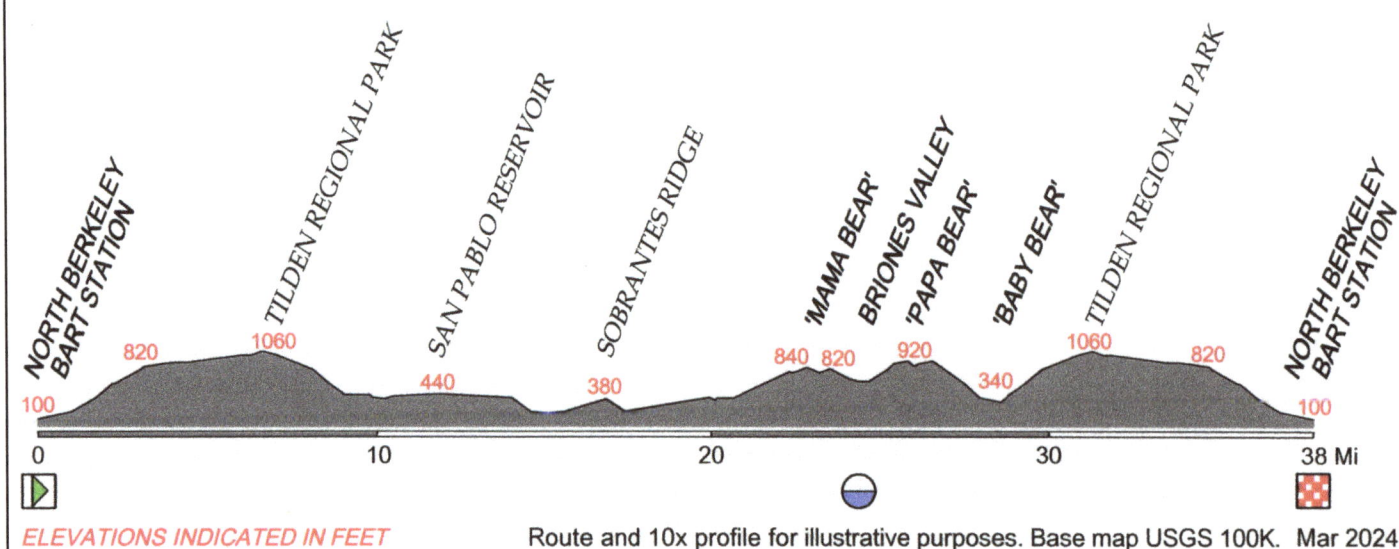

Ride 12: The Three Bears/Briones Valley

This ride is one of the longtime favorite, scenic East Bay routes presenting a medium distance, rolling to hilly 38 mile course through the urban landscape of Berkeley, adjacent parklands and ranches of central Contra Costa County. Many fit riders can complete this popular recreational jaunt or training course in two to three hours.

When weather conditions are clear, cycling over the crest of the Berkeley Hills[31] provides riders some premier expansive, spectacular views of the East Bay shoreline, San Francisco and the pastoral, undeveloped watershed lands of central Contra Costa County. The equally picturesque Pinole Valley and Bear Creek Road offer a combination of easy flat riding, sustained climbs, steep technical descents and potentially hot or windy conditions. This mostly suburban ride guarantees a challenge and includes over 3500 feet of climbing.

The route described begins at the North Berkeley BART Station, then proceeds over the Berkeley Hills through Tilden Regional Park, northwest along San Pablo Reservoir and east along the outskirts of Richmond and Pinole, over Sobrante Ridge. The main part of the ride continues 'clockwise' through the pastoral Pinole Valley and Bear Creek Road ranches, into the watershed lands surrounding Briones and San Pablo Reservoirs.

Bear Creek Road includes three distinct hills known to many local cyclists as *Mama Bear, Papa Bear, and Baby Bear,* which give this ride its alternate names: 'The Three Bears' or simply 'The Bears.'[32] *Mama Bear*, also known as Lawson Hill, is first — followed by the steady climb over *Papa Bear.* A speedy descent to San Pablo Reservoir precedes the short, sharp ramp nicknamed *Baby Bear* and the last part of the ride west to Berkeley. The steep climb through Tilden Regional Park along Wildcat Canyon Road and the hectic ride down Spruce Street into Berkeley make it a tough nine-mile finish. For those returning directly to San Francisco using BART, an alternative to the Wildcat Canyon Road climb is the more gradual two-mile climb south along Camino Pablo to the Orinda BART Station.

Ride Characteristics

Difficulty: Moderate

Distance: 38 miles

Terrain: Some flat, mostly mixed rolling and hilly. Several moderate and steady uphill sections through Berkeley; several short, and several sustained, steep climbs and descents within Tilden and Briones Regional Parks.

Elevation Range: Approximately 100 feet to 1060 feet above sea level.

Climbing: Approx. 3525 feet

Situation: Urban and urban parkland setting; rural segments of two lane highway

Road Conditions: Street traffic, moderate to heavy; pedestrians, moderate to none; road surfaces, good to rough, slippery on foggy or overcast wet morning descents through wooded parklands.

Weather: Sea breezes off the bay and exposure at higher elevations can provide substantial wind factors. Morning conditions can often be cool and cloudy. Summer and Fall afternoon temperatures can be hot.

[31] Reaching elevations above 1000 feet along Wildcat Canyon Road in Tilden Regional Park.
[32] The three climbs are in the 6 – 7% range. *Baby Bear* climbs 80 feet in just a quarter mile. *Mama Bear* and *Papa Bear* climb 300 and 360 feet, respectively, each in about one mile.

Notes: Bike shops numbered 36 through 38 and 43 through 44 in Appendix 1 are found in the general vicinity traversed along this route through Berkeley and Contra Costa County. Nevertheless, shops are not always open or nearby — carrying essential tools, a pump, a tire repair kit and 2 tubes is highly recommended. This ride also includes significant segments of park road and rural road where there are *no* services.

Approximate Ride Time: 2 to 3 hours.

Detailed Route Directions

Leave the North Berkeley BART Station; cross to Sacramento Street and begin riding north on Sacramento Street to Hopkins Street. Turn right on Hopkins Street and proceed one block to Monterey Avenue. Turn left on Monterey Avenue and begin climbing steadily to Marin Avenue. Bear right on Marin Avenue and continue climbing to the Arlington Circle.

Proceed around the Arlington Circle counter clockwise — past Del Norte Street — and bear right on Los Angeles Avenue. Climb four steep blocks to Spruce Street. Turn left on Spruce Street and continuing climbing steadily, eventually reaching Grizzly Peak Boulevard. Cross Grizzly Peak Boulevard and enter Tilden Regional Park on Wildcat Canyon Road.

Wildcat Canyon Road, Tilden Regional Park

Follow the mostly flat and winding Wildcat Canyon Road through the park, past Lake Anza and the Brazil Room. Descend quickly past the Botanical Garden and bear left at South Park Drive. Begin the gradual but steady climb on Wildcat Canyon Road to Inspiration Point, the ride's highest elevation, at 1060 feet. The road flattens out briefly at the parking lot before beginning a steep and technical 2.5 mile descent to its intersection with San Pablo Dam Road, Bear Creek Road and Camino Pablo.

Opposite: San Pablo Reservoir (u) and Castro Ranch Road (l)

Turn left on San Pablo Dam Road and ride northwest through the rolling terrain west of San Pablo Reservoir, which eventually descends to Castro Ranch Road. Turn right on Castro Ranch Road, climb gradually over Sobrante Ridge, through the Carriage Hills subdivision and then descend rapidly to Alhambra Valley Road. Turn right on Alhambra Valley Road and continue to Bear Creek Road. Turn right on Bear Creek Road and ride past adjacent the horse farms and ranch lands to the base of Lawson Hill, or *Mama Bear*. Climb steadily over the 840-foot *Mama Bear,* and then descend to the entrance of Briones Regional Park at Briones Valley Road — destination point of the ride.

Briones Regional Park is a logical place for a rest stop. Turn left and use Briones Valley Road to enter and leave the park. Some cyclists bypass the park — continuing on Bear Creek Road, climbing steadily over the 920-foot *Papa Bear* before a rapid, sinuous two-mile descent to *Baby Bear*, the short but abrupt 80 foot rise to the intersection of Bear Creek Road, Camino Pablo, San Pablo Dam Road and Wildcat Canyon Road. Many riders select their lowest gear as they cross the small bridge over San Pablo Creek *before* the road steepens sharply, but whether spinning or grinding the gears, *Baby Bear* is brief — over in less than five minutes. The last sustained climbing still lies ahead.

Cross San Pablo Dam Road and begin climbing steeply and steadily, 2.5 miles along Wildcat Canyon Road to Inspiration Point in Tilden Regional Park. Descend to the Botanical Garden, past South Park Drive, where a last short rise awaits. Climb past the Brazil Room and ride along the flat section of Wildcat Canyon Road to the park exit at Grizzly Peak Boulevard.

Cross to Spruce Street and begin the steady, rapid descent into Berkeley. Watch for buses, cars, and pedestrians, along this busy, winding, downhill section of Spruce Street, particularly after crossing Marin Avenue and approaching the intersection of Spruce Street and Los Angeles Avenue. Turn right on Los Angeles Avenue and quickly descend to the Arlington Circle. Continue counterclockwise around the circle and bear right on to Marin Avenue, then ride just over one block to Monterey Avenue.

Bear left on Monterey Avenue and descend gradually to Hopkins Street. Turn right on Hopkins Street and proceed one block to Sacramento Street. Turn left on Sacramento Street and continue to Virginia Street, where the ride ends at the North Berkeley BART Station.

Opposite: Briones Reservoir / Bear Creek Road ('Mama Bear')

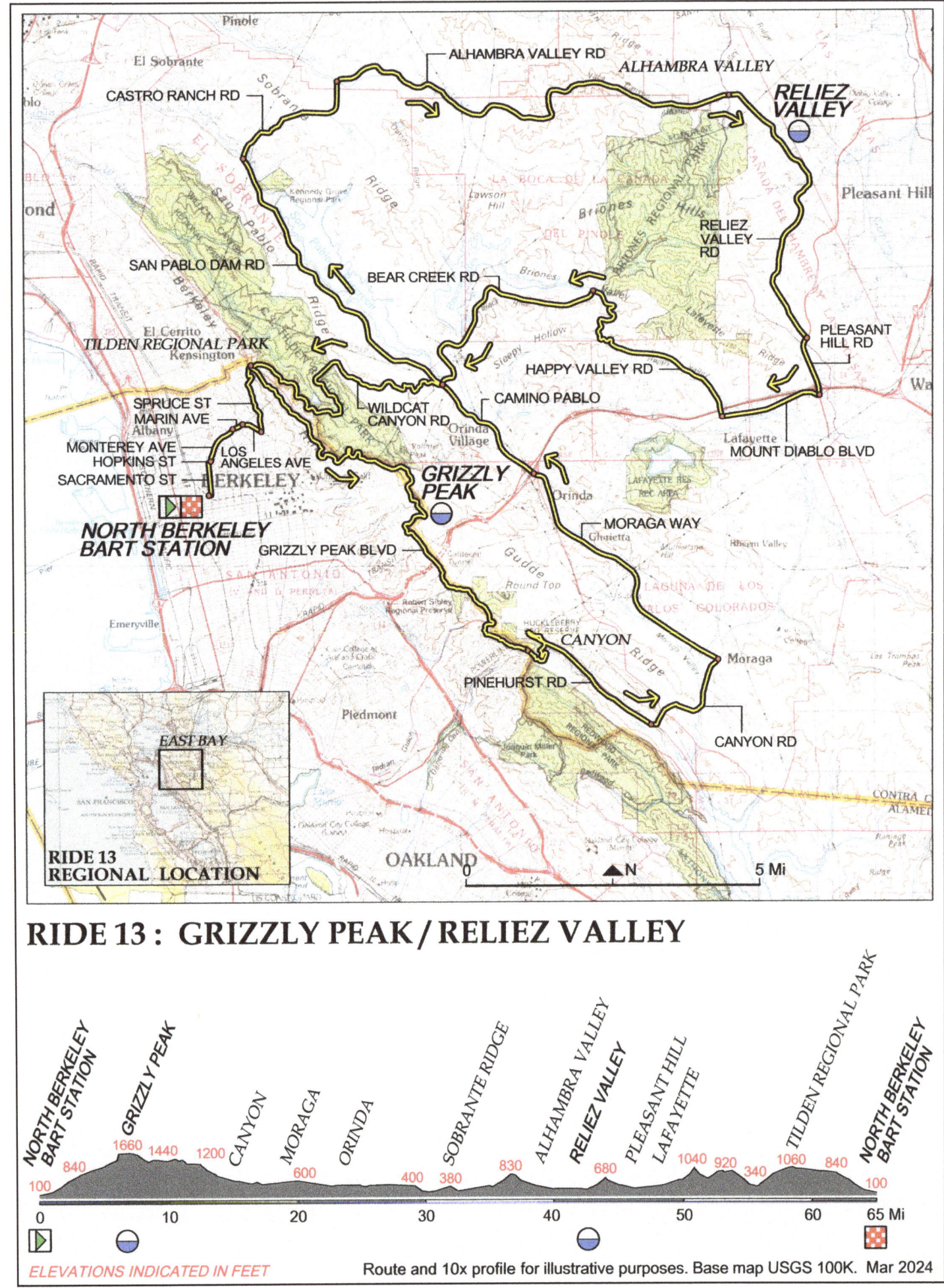

RIDE 13 : GRIZZLY PEAK / RELIEZ VALLEY

ELEVATIONS INDICATED IN FEET — Route and 10x profile for illustrative purposes. Base map USGS 100K. Mar 2024

Ride 13: Grizzly Peak/Reliez Valley

This is an East Bay ride that presents a medium distance, rolling to hilly, picturesque course through the urban landscapes of Berkeley and Oakland, their suburbs and the adjacent ranch and parklands of central Contra Costa County. A serious challenge, one that follows familiar roads often included in regular rides of the East Bay's venerable bike clubs,[33] the course covers about 65 mostly suburban miles. Fit riders will need three to four hours to complete the full ride from North Berkeley. This ride is strenuous and includes about 5400 feet of climbing. There are steep, technical descents and sometimes hot or windy conditions. Nevertheless, the hilly route remains popular for many — the sustained efforts and 'tough-going' seem to increase the 'payback' quality of the ridgeline views and the overall sense of accomplishment that comes from completing this ride.

After beginning at the North Berkeley BART Station, riders climb steadily through Berkeley to the crest of the Berkeley Hills, then along Grizzly Peak Boulevard and Skyline Boulevard in the Oakland Highlands, northwest of Redwood Regional Park. After a steep, rapid descent on the infamous Pinehurst Road,[34] riders pass though the hamlet of Canyon and eventually reach the City of Moraga. There, the course continues along rolling roads through Orinda and west of San Pablo Reservoir to the outskirts of Richmond. Suburban scenery quickly becomes rural as riders climb over Sobrante Ridge and into Pinole Valley.

After several flatter miles alongside Pinole Creek, Alhambra Valley Road gives riders an abrupt climb and a winding alignment through Vaca Canyon and into Alhambra Valley, where the course reaches the outskirts of the City of Martinez. Here, Reliez Valley Road begins the return ride through Pleasant Hill and Lafayette. Riders eventually climb over Happy Valley Road before descending into the Briones Valley. After climbing *'Papa Bear'* [35] along Bear Creek Road, a speedy descent to San Pablo Reservoir precedes the short, sharp ramp nicknamed *Baby Bear* and the last part of the ride west to Berkeley. The steep climb through Tilden Regional Park along Wildcat Canyon Road and the hectic ride down Spruce Street into Berkeley make it a tough nine-mile finish. For those returning directly to San Francisco using BART, an alternative to the Wildcat Canyon Road climb is a more gradual two-mile climb south along Camino Pablo to the Orinda BART Station.

Ride Characteristics
Difficulty: Moderate
Distance: 65 miles
Terrain: Some flat, mostly mixed rolling and hilly. Several moderate and steady uphill sections through Berkeley and Oakland; several short and several sustained steep climbs and descents along Pinehurst Road, Alhambra Valley Road, Reliez Valley Road and Happy Valley Road, as well as through Briones and Tilden Regional Parks.
Elevation Range: Approximately 12 feet to 1660 feet above sea level.
Climbing: Approx. 5380 feet

---

[33] Riders of the *Berkeley Bicycle Club* and the *Grizzly Peak Cyclists* are familiar faces in this region. GPC sponsored the first *Grizzly Peak Century* ride event in 1975.
[34] Pinehurst Road presents a narrow, winding, steep 1.25 mile, 400 foot descent past Eastport, followed by a more gradual 2.5 mile, 300 foot decline through Canyon alongside San Leandro Creek.
[35] Approx. 960 feet elevation.

Situation: Urban and urban parkland setting; rural segments of two lane highway.

Road Conditions: Street traffic, moderate to heavy; pedestrians, moderate to none; road surfaces, good to rough, slippery on foggy or overcast wet morning descents through wooded parklands.

Weather: Sea breezes off the bay and exposure at higher elevations can provide substantial wind factors. Morning conditions can often be cool and cloudy. Summer and Fall afternoon temperatures can be hot.

Notes: Bike shops numbered 36 through 45 and 48 through 51 in Appendix 1 are found in the general vicinity traversed along this route through Berkeley and Contra Costa County. Nevertheless, shops are not always open or nearby — carrying essential tools, a pump, a tire repair kit and 2 tubes is highly recommended. This ride also includes significant segments of park road and rural road where there are *no* services.

Approximate ride time: 3 to 4 hours.

Detailed Route Directions

Leave the North Berkeley BART Station; cross to Sacramento Street and begin riding north on Sacramento Street to Hopkins Street. Turn right on Hopkins Street and proceed one block to Monterey Avenue. Turn left on Monterey Avenue and begin climbing to Marin Avenue. Bear right on Marin Avenue and continue climbing to the Arlington Circle.

Proceed around the Arlington Circle counter clockwise — past Del Norte Street — and bear right on Los Angeles Avenue. Climb four steep blocks to Spruce Street. Turn left on Spruce Street and continuing climbing steadily, eventually reaching Grizzly Peak Boulevard.

Turn right on Grizzly Peak Boulevard and begin climbing several miles towards the crest of the Berkeley Hills above Claremont Canyon. This part of Grizzly Peak Boulevard combines formidable uphill switchbacks with remarkable panoramic views west near the summit. Descend along the ridgeline to the Robert Sibley Regional Preserve in the highlands of Oakland, where Grizzly Peak Boulevard intersects Skyline Boulevard. Turn left on Skyline Boulevard and continue southeast towards Redwood Regional Park and Pinehurst Road.

Bear left on to Pinehurst Road and begin a very steep, technical 1.25 mile descent with hairpin turns to Eastport, where a final switchback begins a more gradual 2.5 mile downhill section of Pinehurst Road, passing through the hamlet of Canyon before reaching Canyon Road. Turn left on Canyon Road and ride to Moraga Way in central Moraga.

Turn left on Moraga Way and ride five miles to Camino Pablo in the City of Orinda. Bear left on Camino Pablo and continue to the intersection of Wildcat Canyon Road, Bear Creek Road and San Pablo Dam Road. Ride northwest along San Pablo Dam Road through the rolling terrain west of San Pablo Reservoir, which eventually descends to Castro Ranch Road. Turn right on Castro Ranch Road, climb gradually over Sobrante Ridge, through the Carriage Hills subdivision and then descend rapidly to Alhambra Valley Road. Turn right on Alhambra Valley Road and continue to Bear Creek Road.

Cross Bear Creek Road and continue on Alhambra Valley Road, over the infamous 'Pig Farm Hill'[36] and through Vaca Canyon, into the Alhambra Valley and the outskirts of the City of Martinez. Bear right on to Reliez Valley Road — destination point of the ride.

---

[36] The pig farm is long gone but formerly added an unforgettable, odorous punch to this short but steep and strenuous segment of Alhambra Valley Road.

Opposite: Reliez Valley Road

Alhambra Valley Road / 'Pig Farm Hill'

Happy Valley Road

Briones Reservoir at Bear Creek Raod ('Papa Bear')

Begin the return by continuing south on Reliez Valley Road to Pleasant Hill Road. Turn right and follow Pleasant Hill Road to Mount Diablo Boulevard. Turn right and ride along Mount Diablo Boulevard through the City of Lafayette to Happy Valley Road. Turn right and proceed on Happy Valley Road, climbing gradually, then steeply to about 900 feet elevation, before a winding descent to Bear Creek Road.

Turn left on to Bear Creek Road and climb steadily over the 920-foot *Papa Bear* before a rapid, sinuous two-mile descent to *Baby Bear*, the short but abrupt 80 foot rise to the intersection of Bear Creek Road, Camino Pablo, San Pablo Dam Road and Wildcat Canyon Road. Many riders select their lowest gear as they cross the small bridge over San Pablo Creek *before* the road steepens sharply, but whether spinning or grinding the gears, *Baby Bear* is brief — over in less than five minutes. The last sustained climbing still lies ahead.

Cross San Pablo Dam Road and begin climbing steeply and steadily, 2.5 miles along Wildcat Canyon Road to Inspiration Point in Tilden Regional Park. Descend to the Botanical Garden, past South Park Drive, where a last short rise awaits. Climb past the Brazil Room and ride along the flat section of Wildcat Canyon Road to the park exit at Grizzly Peak Boulevard.

Cross to Spruce Street and begin the steady, rapid descent into Berkeley. Watch for buses, cars, and pedestrians, along this busy, winding, downhill section of Spruce Street, particularly after crossing Marin Avenue and approaching the intersection of Spruce Street and Los Angeles Avenue. Turn right on Los Angeles Avenue and quickly descend to the Arlington Circle. Continue counterclockwise around the circle and bear right on to Marin Avenue, then ride just over one block to Monterey Avenue.

Bear left on Monterey Avenue and descend gradually to Hopkins Street. Turn right on Hopkins Street and proceed one block to Sacramento Street. Turn left on Sacramento Street and continue to Virginia Street, where the ride ends at the North Berkeley BART Station.

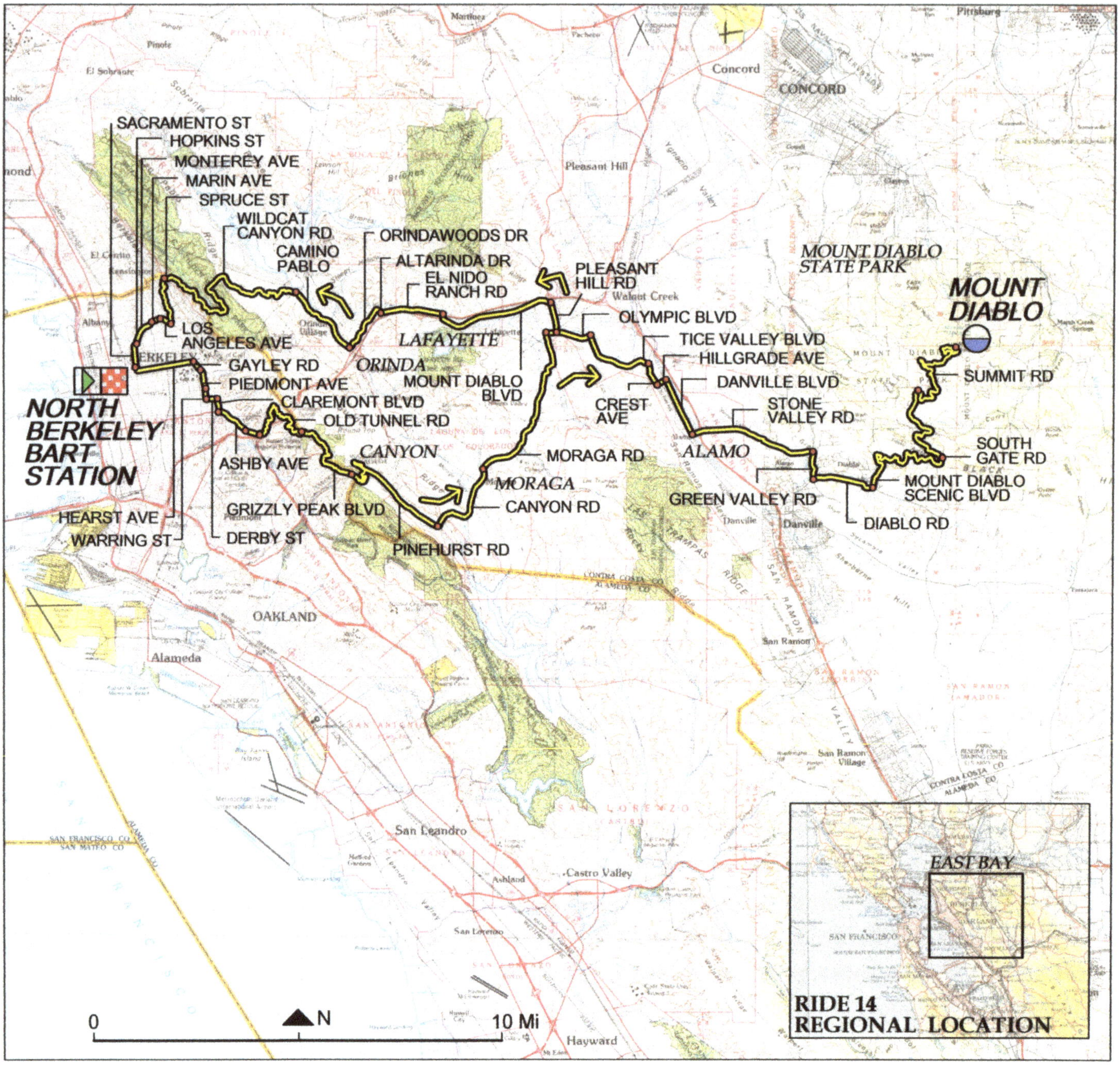

RIDE 14 : MOUNT DIABLO

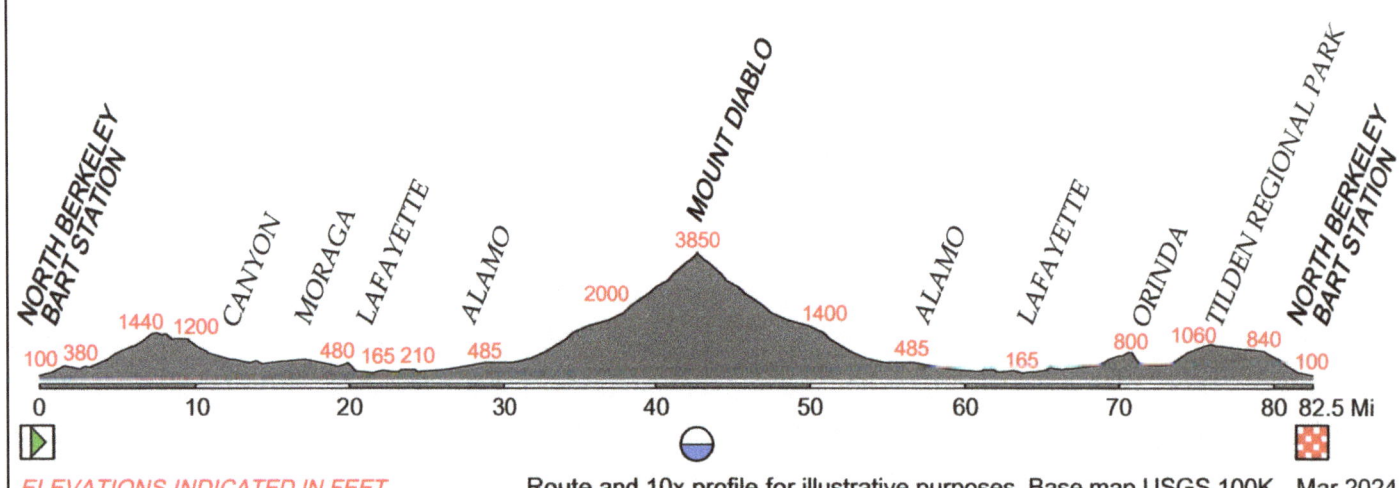

ELEVATIONS INDICATED IN FEET

Route and 10x profile for illustrative purposes. Base map USGS 100K. Mar 2024

Ride 14: Mount Diablo

This ride is a longtime favorite for bicycling climbers of all categories. The route from North Berkeley presents an ambitious 82.5 mile course through the urban landscapes of Berkeley and central Contra Costa County, ultimately reaching the summit of Mount Diablo — second highest peak in the Bay Area — at 3850 feet. Whether starting the ride from the nearest BART station or by riding over the crest of the Berkeley Hills, cyclists are undertaking one of the toughest hill climbs in the entire San Francisco region — just the 12 mile climb to the peak gains over 3300 feet of elevation and requires an hour or more for many fit cyclists.

The complete ride from Berkeley includes over 7200 feet of climbing. It's an all-day affair for most riders, especially if heat and headwinds become a factor. Unlike Marin County's Mount Tamalpais, which has some shade and flat sections of road, Mount Diablo is largely exposed and requires a sustained effort during the entire climb. There are flat sections, but the incline is mostly relentless and culminates with a 600 foot ramp of 18% gradient at the summit. Cyclists reach an elevation close to 4000 feet, above nearly *everything* else in the Bay Area! The views from the peak on a clear day are spectacular in every direction. The fast and technical descent is also great 'payback' for the effort made to get there.

The route described begins at the North Berkeley BART Station, however, this ride can also be staged from other East Bay BART stations, depending on rider preference.[37] The North Berkeley route proceeds south and east over the crest of the Berkeley Hills. After a steep, rapid descent on the infamous Pinehurst Road,[38] riders pass though the hamlet of Canyon and eventually reach the City of Moraga. There, the course continues towards Lafayette, through Tice Valley to Danville Boulevard and south to Alamo.

Mostly flat riding through Stone Valley and Green Valley leads to the southern entrance of Mount Diablo State Park, where the traditional Mount Diablo 'South Gate' hill climb really begins. A steep and steady grind along a combination of Mount Diablo Scenic Boulevard, South Gate Road and Summit Road eventually reaches the summit.

The return course between Mount Diablo's summit and Lafayette is essentially the reverse of the approach directions. Riders can opt to finish the ride at the Lafayette BART Station or continue west, parallel to Highway 24 towards Orinda, where they can either finish the ride at the Orinda BART Station or choose to continue riding further north via Camino Pablo, eventually climbing Wildcat Canyon Road through Tilden Regional Park and descending into Berkeley to finish the full ride at the North Berkeley BART Station.

Ride Characteristics

Difficulty: High

Distance: 82.5 miles

Terrain: Some flat, mostly rolling and hilly. Several moderate and steady uphill sections through the Berkeley and Oakland hills. Sustained steep descent along Pinehurst Road. Sustained steep climb and descent along South Gate Road within Mount Diablo State Park. Sustained steep climb along Wildcat Canyon Road within Tilden Regional Park.

---

[37] Both the Orinda and Lafayette BART Stations are conveniently located along this route.

[38] Pinehurst Road presents a narrow, winding, steep 1.25 mile, 400 foot descent past Eastport, followed by a more gradual 2.5 mile, 300 foot decline through Canyon alongside San Leandro Creek.

Elevation Range: Approximately 100 feet to 3850 feet above sea level.
Climbing: Approx. 7230 feet
Situation: Urban and urban parkland setting; rural segments of two lane highway.
Road Conditions: Street traffic, moderate to heavy; pedestrians, moderate to none; road surfaces, good to rough, slippery on foggy or overcast wet morning descents through wooded parklands.
Weather: Sea breezes off the bay and mountain exposure at higher elevations can provide substantial wind factors. Morning conditions can often be cool and cloudy. Summer and Fall afternoon temperatures can be hot.
Notes: Bike shops numbered 36 through 45 and 47 through 51 in Appendix 1 are found in the general vicinity traversed along this route through Berkeley and Contra Costa County. Nevertheless, shops are not always open or nearby — carrying essential tools, a pump, a tire repair kit and 2 tubes is highly recommended. This ride also includes lengthy segments of State Park road where there are *no* services.
Approximate Ride Time: 5 hours.

Detailed Route Directions

Leave the North Berkeley BART Station; cross to Sacramento Street and ride south on Sacramento Street one block to Hearst Avenue. Turn left on Hearst Avenue and ride along the Ohlone Greenway, climbing gradually past Martin Luther King Jr. Way and Shattuck Avenue to Oxford Street. Turn right on Oxford Street and ride two blocks to University Avenue. Turn left at University Avenue and enter the University of California, Berkeley campus by climbing the short rise up Crescent Drive to University Drive. Turn left on University Drive and ride through the wooded campus, climbing steadily to Gayley Road near the Greek Theater and Memorial Stadium.

Turn right on Gayley Road and ride past the Greek Theater to Stadium Rim Way, where Gayley Road becomes Piedmont Avenue. Descend on Piedmont Avenue to its merge with Warring Street. Bear right on to Warring Street and continue to Derby Street. Turn left on Derby Street and ride to Belrose Avenue. Turn right on Belrose Avenue and ride one block to its merge with Claremont Boulevard. Continue on Claremont Boulevard two blocks to Claremont Avenue. Turn right on Claremont Avenue and ride one block to Ashby Avenue.

Turn left on Ashby Avenue, which becomes Tunnel Road as you leave the Berkeley city limits. Continue past the Claremont Hotel, beginning the steady climb to the ridgeline above. Continue on Tunnel Road, climbing to its merge with the on and off-ramps for Highway 24 and southbound Highway 13. Use caution and turn left, crossing the highway ramps. Continue on Tunnel Road, now climbing more steadily towards Caldecott Lane. Turn left and climb one block, then turn right to remain on Tunel Road. Pass the Emergency Preparedness Center and begin the steady, winding climb — at first gradual, then steepening as you approach the old Caldecott Tunnel entrance.[39]

Once past the old tunnel entrance Tunnel Road becomes Skyline Boulevard. Continue the winding climb along Skyline Boulevard, past Grizzly Peak Boulevard and the Robert Sibley Regional Preserve, to its intersection with Pinehurst Road near Redwood Regional Park.

---

[39] The original Caldecott Tunnel was abandoned after its replacement by the modern system of tunnels built along the current alignment of Highway 24.

Opposite: Climbing South Gate Road, Mount Diablo State Park

Bear left on to Pinehurst Road and begin a very steep, technical 1.25 mile descent with hairpin turns to Eastport, where a final switchback begins a more gradual 2.5 mile downhill section of Pinehurst Road, passing through the hamlet of Canyon before reaching Canyon Road. Turn left on Canyon Road and ride to Moraga Way in central Moraga.

Cross the intersection at Moraga *Way* and ride northeast on Moraga *Road* to Saint Mary's Road. Turn right on Saint Mary's Road and continue to Glenside Drive in Lafayette. Turn right on Glenside Drive and ride to Reliez Station Road. Bear right on Reliez Station Road and continue to Olympic Boulevard. Turn right on Olympic Boulevard and ride to Tice Valley Boulevard in Walnut Creek. Turn right on Tice Valley Boulevard and continue to Crest Avenue. Turn right on Crest Avenue and ride to Hillgrade Avenue. Turn left on Hillgrade Avenue and ride to Danville Boulevard. Turn right on Danville Boulevard and continue to Stone Valley Road in central Alamo. Turn left on Stone Valley Road and ride to Green Valley Road. Turn right on Green Valley Road and ride to Diablo Road. Turn left on Diablo Road and continue to Mount Diablo Scenic Boulevard.

Turn left on Mount Diablo Scenic Boulevard and find a nearby location to take a short break. Of course, shade is preferable if it's hot. Many a cyclist will take this opportunity to eat, drink and stretch for a few minutes. Continue north on Mount Diablo Scenic Boulevard and begin the winding climb to South Gate Road at the entrance to Mount Diablo State Park. Continue on South Gate Road, climbing steeply to the ranger residence, then steadily to Rock City. At Rock City, the road steepens and includes several switchbacks leading to a flatter climbing section before the intersection of South Gate Road, North Gate Road, and Summit Road.[40] Turn right on Summit Road and continue climbing steeply through another series of switchbacks preceding the final short, extremely steep, ramp to the summit parking lot and the Mount Diablo Lighthouse — destination and turnaround point of the ride.

The descent and return ride from the top of Mount Diablo is straightforward — mostly following the reverse of the route directions for the climb. The Summit Road downhill from the parking lot is quick and becomes technical right away as you backtrack through tight switchback turns to South Gate Road. Turn left on South Gate Road and roll past the Junction Ranger Station descending first along a section of ridgeline, then steeply down another section of switchbacks to Rock City. Continue through Rock City southeast along Fossil Ridge before passing the Ranger Residence and beginning the last steep descent out of the State Park where South Gate Road meets Mount Diablo Scenic Boulevard. Continue out of the park and southerly on Mount Diablo Scenic Boulevard to Diablo Road.

Turn right on Diablo Road and ride to Road to Green Valley Road. Turn right on Green Valley Road and ride to Stone Valley Road. Turn left on Stone Valley Road and continue through Alamo, eventually reaching Danville Boulevard.

Turn right on Danville Boulevard and ride to Hillgrade Avenue. Turn left on Hillgrade Avenue and proceed three blocks to Crest Avenue. Bear right on Crest Avenue and ride to Tice Valley Road. Turn left on Tice Valley Road and ride to Olympic Boulevard. Turn left on Olympic Boulevard and continue to Pleasant Hill Road. Turn right on Pleasant Hill road and continue to Mount Diablo Boulevard in Lafayette.

[40] Location of the Junction Ranger Station.

Opposite:
Summit Road, Mount Diablo (u), / Mount Diablo Light House (c) / Mount Diablo South Panorama (l)

Turn left on Mount Diablo Boulevard and continue through Lafayette to Happy Valley Road. If returning to San Francisco from Lafayette's BART Station, turn right on Happy Valley Road. Cross through the Highway 24 underpass and proceed into the station. If continuing the ride west, follow Mount Diablo Boulevard to El Nido Ranch Road.

Bear right on El Nido Ranch Road and cross through the Highway 24 underpass before continuing west to Saint Stephen's Drive, where the El Nido Ranch Road becomes Altarinda Drive. Follow Altarinda Drive past the Orinda city offices to Orindawoods Drive. Bear left on to Orindawoods Drive and descend past the Orinda School, where Orindawoods Drive first becomes Altarinda *Road* and then becomes Santa Maria Way for several blocks before descending steeply to Orinda Way.

If returning to San Francisco from Orinda's BART Station turn left on Orinda Way and ride a hundred feet or so the entrance of the bicycle and pedestrian bridge to the Orinda Station. Continue along the path to the parking lot and station entrance.

If completing the full ride back to Berkeley, continue on Santa Maria Way one block, past Orinda Way to Camino Pablo. Turn right on Camino Pablo and ride northwest to Wildcat Canyon Road. Turn left and begin climbing steeply and steadily, 2.5 miles along Wildcat Canyon Road to Inspiration Point in Tilden Regional Park. Descend to the Botanical Garden, past South Park Drive, where a last short rise awaits. Climb past the Brazil Room and ride along the flat section of Wildcat Canyon Road to the park exit at Grizzly Peak Boulevard.

Cross to Spruce Street and begin the steady, rapid descent into Berkeley. Watch for buses, cars, and pedestrians, along this busy, winding, downhill section of Spruce Street, particularly after crossing Marin Avenue and approaching the intersection of Spruce Street and Los Angeles Avenue. Turn right on Los Angeles Avenue and quickly descend to the Arlington Circle. Continue counterclockwise around the circle and bear right on Marin Avenue, then ride just over one block to Monterey Avenue.

Bear left on Monterey Avenue and descend gradually to Hopkins Street. Turn right on Hopkins Street and proceed one block to Sacramento Street. Turn left on Sacramento Street and continue to Virginia Street, where the ride ends at the North Berkeley BART Station.

Opposite: Looking at return route along Summit Road, Mount Diablo

RIDE 15 : MORGAN TERRITORY PRESERVE

ELEVATIONS INDICATED IN FEET

Route and 10x profile for illustrative purposes. Base map USGS 100K. Mar 2024

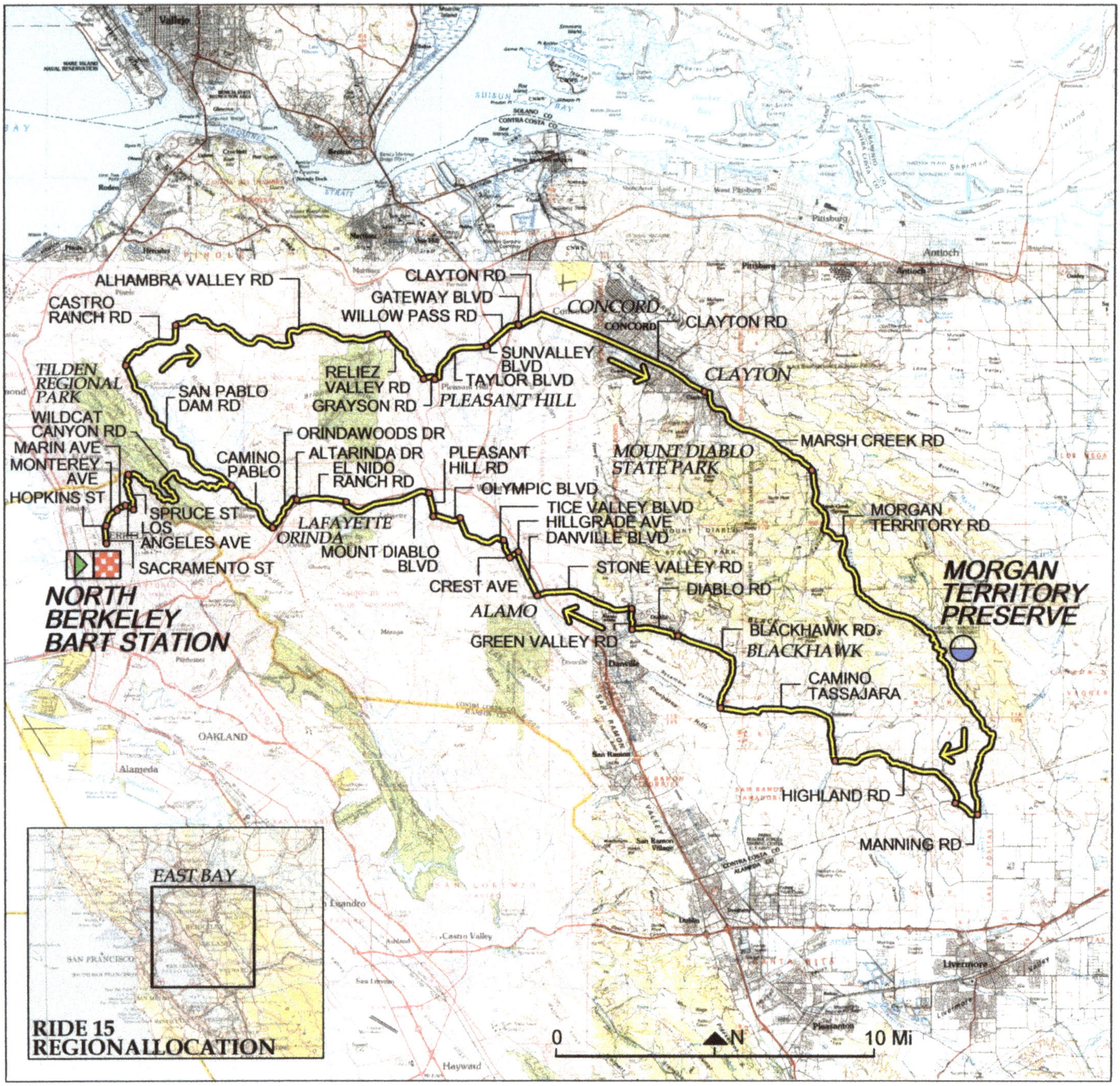

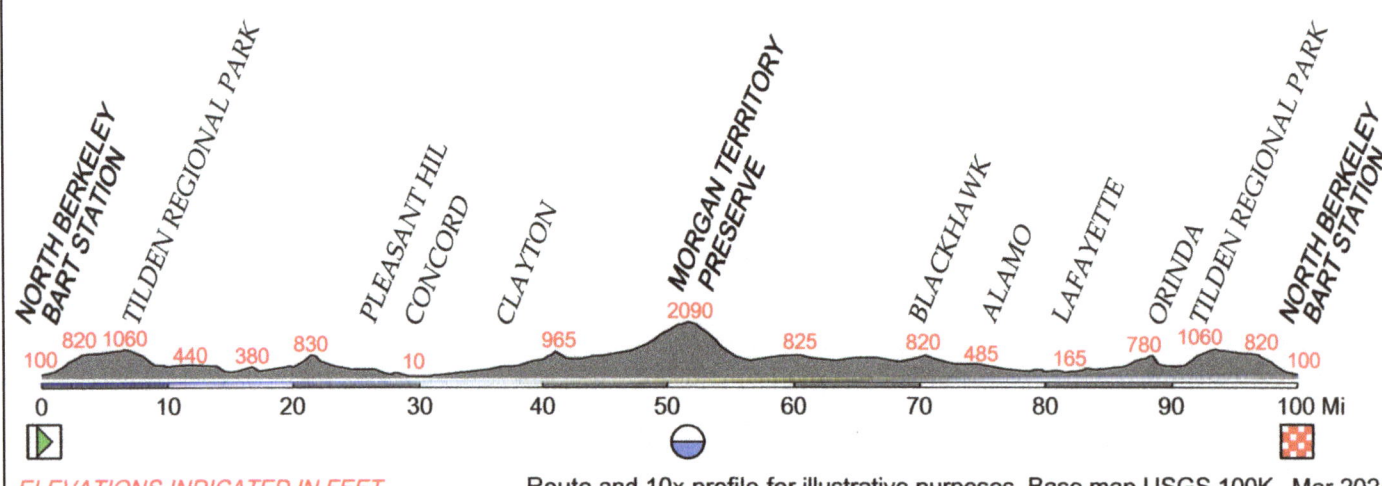

Ride 15: Morgan Territory Preserve

This ride presents a long distance, rolling and hilly course through the suburban landscapes north of Berkeley and into the adjacent ranch and parklands east of Concord. Riders traverse central Contra Costa County in an ambitious training ride or tour covering 100 miles. Most fit cyclists will need over five hours to complete the full ride — returning to North Berkeley. There are no lighthouses, but it's every bit as challenging as the Point Reyes Peninsula ride — combining long distance, 5600 feet of climbing and often hot or windy conditions. Without a doubt, this is one of the East Bay's toughest rides — a 'clockwise' loop around Mount Diablo.

The route described begins at the North Berkeley BART Station but this ride can also be staged from other East Bay BART stations, depending on rider preference.[41] The North Berkeley course climbs over the Berkeley Hills and continues northwest past Richmond, then east to the outskirts of Martinez, and through Concord to Clayton. There, riders proceed southeast to Morgan Territory Road and continue nine miles along the narrow, rough ranch road, steadily climbing the eastern flank of Mount Diablo to an elevation just under 2100 feet at the Morgan Territory Regional Preserve — destination of the ride.

The return begins with a rapid, technical five mile descent to the outskirts of the City of Livermore, then follows rolling farmland roads west, reaching the communities of Blackhawk and Alamo, where wide boulevards and suburban riding replace two-lane roads and pastoral views.

Between Alamo and North Berkeley, the return ride follows the same course described for the Mount Diablo ride — north through the San Ramon Valley to Lafayette and west towards Orinda and Berkeley. Riders can opt to finish the ride at the Lafayette BART Station or continue west, parallel to Highway 24 towards Orinda, where they can either finish the ride at the Orinda BART Station or choose to continue further north via Camino Pablo, eventually climbing Wildcat Canyon Road through Tilden Regional Park and descending into Berkeley to finish the full ride at the North Berkeley BART Station.

Ride Characteristics
Difficulty: High
Distance: 100 miles
Terrain: Some flat, mostly mixed rolling and hilly. Moderate and steady uphill section through Berkeley. Several short, steep climbs and descents along Alhambra Valley Road and Reliez Valley Road. Two sustained steep climbs, the first along Morgan Territory Road and the second, along Wildcat Canyon Road within Tilden Regional Park.
Elevation Range: Approximately 10 feet to 2100 feet above sea level.
Climbing: Approx. 5665 feet
Situation: Urban and urban parkland setting; rural segments of two-lane highway.
Road Conditions: Street traffic, moderate to heavy; pedestrians, moderate to none; road surfaces, mostly good to very rough on the narrow, one-lane segment of Morgan Ter-

---

[41] The Orinda, Lafayette and Concord BART Stations are located along this route.

ritory Road north of the Regional Preserve; slippery on foggy or overcast wet morning descents through wooded parklands.

Weather: Sea breezes off the bay and exposure at higher elevations can provide substantial wind factors. Morning conditions can often be cool and cloudy. Summer and Fall afternoon temperatures can be hot.

Notes: Bike shops numbered 36 through 51 in Appendix 1 are found in the general vicinity traversed along this route through Berkeley and Contra Costa County. Nevertheless, shops are not always open or nearby — carrying essential tools, a pump, a tire repair kit and 2 tubes is highly recommended. This ride also includes lengthy segments of rural road where there are *no* services.

Approximate Ride Time: 5 to 6 hours.

Detailed Route Directions

Leave the North Berkeley BART Station; cross to Sacramento Street and begin riding north on Sacramento Street to Hopkins Street. Turn right on Hopkins Street and proceed one block to Monterey Avenue. Turn left on Monterey Avenue and begin climbing steadily to Marin Avenue. Bear right on Marin Avenue and continue climbing to the Arlington Circle.

Proceed around the Arlington Circle counter clockwise — past Del Norte Street — and bear right on Los Angeles Avenue. Climb four steep blocks to Spruce Street. Turn left on Spruce Street and continuing climbing steadily, eventually reaching Grizzly Peak Boulevard. Cross Grizzly Peak Boulevard and enter Tilden Regional Park on Wildcat Canyon Road.

Follow the mostly flat and winding Wildcat Canyon Road through the park, past Lake Anza and the Brazil Room. Descend quickly past the Botanical Garden and bear left at South Park Drive. Begin the gradual but steady climb on Wildcat Canyon Road to Inspiration Point, the ride's highest elevation, at 1060 feet. The road flattens out briefly at the parking lot before beginning a steep and technical 2.5 mile descent to its intersection with San Pablo Dam Road, Bear Creek Road and Camino Pablo.

Turn left on San Pablo Dam Road and ride northwest through the rolling terrain west of San Pablo Reservoir, which eventually descends to Castro Ranch Road. Turn right on Castro Ranch Road, climb gradually over Sobrante Ridge, through the Carriage Hills subdi-

Morgan Territory Regional Preserve entrance

Cresting Morgan Territory Road

vision and then descend rapidly to Alhambra Valley Road. Turn right on Alhambra Valley Road and continue to Bear Creek Road.

Cross Bear Creek Road and continue on Alhambra Valley Road, over the infamous 'Pig Farm Hill' and through Vaca Canyon, into the Alhambra Valley and the outskirts of the City of Martinez. Bear right on to Reliez Valley Road and begin gradually climbing to Grayson Road. Turn left on Grayson Road and ride several blocks to Taylor Boulevard. Turn left on Taylor Boulevard and continue north through the City of Pleasant Hill.

Taylor Boulevard becomes Sun Valley Boulevard as riders pass the Sun Valley Mall near Highway 680. Continue on Sun Valley Boulevard through the Highway 680 underpass, where Sun Valley Boulevard becomes Willow Pass Road. Follow Willow Pass Road through the Highway 242 underpass and past Market Street to Gateway Boulevard. Bear right on Gateway Boulevard and proceed one block to Clayton Road. Turn left on Clayton Road and continue to Colfax Street and Sunset Avenue, in downtown Concord.

Bear right at Colfax Street to remain on Clayton Road. Ride past the Concord BART Station and southeast, away from central Concord. Continue for six miles along the straight and flat Clayton Road, eventually rising gradually towards the town of Clayton. Clayton

Descending Morgan Territory Road (towards Livermore Valley)

Road intersects Marsh Creek Road near the center of town. Turn right on Marsh Creek Road and continue about four miles to Morgan Territory Road.

The next section presents the main namesake part of the ride. Bear right on Morgan Territory Road and ride just over nine miles through the horse ranches and farms, climbing gradually, then steeply, over the sometimes rough road surface into the Morgan Territory Regional Preserve. A portion of the road is one-lane wide. The equestrian staging area and parking lot near the crest of Morgan Territory Road provide a convenient place for a rest stop and destination point of the ride.

The fifty mile return begins on the flat upper section of Morgan Territory Road and then quickly descends about 1000 feet to the outskirts of Livermore. Use caution on the technical turns but enjoy the 5.5 mile downhill to Manning Road as 'payback' for the tough climbing thus far. Turn right on Manning Road and begin the flat trek west, proceeding to Highland Road. Turn right on Highland Road and continue to Camino Tassajara.

Turn right on Camino Tassajara and ride to Blackhawk Road. Turn right on Blackhawk Road and continue through Blackhawk to the community of Diablo, where Blackhawk Road becomes Diablo Road, west of Mount Diablo Scenic Boulevard.

Continue on Diablo Road to its intersection with Green Valley Road. Turn right on Green Valley Road and ride to Stone Valley Road. Turn left on Stone Valley Road and continue through Alamo, eventually reaching Danville Boulevard and the center of Alamo.

Turn right on Danville Boulevard and ride to Hillgrade Avenue. Turn left on Hillgrade Avenue and proceed three blocks to Crest Avenue. Bear right on Crest Avenue and ride to Tice Valley Road. Turn left on Tice Valley Road and ride to Olympic Boulevard. Turn left on Olympic Boulevard and continue to Pleasant Hill Road. Turn right on Pleasant Hill road and ride to Mount Diablo Boulevard in Lafayette.

Turn left on Mount Diablo Boulevard and continue to Happy Valley Road. If returning to San Francisco from Lafayette's BART Station, turn right on Happy Valley Road. Cross through the Highway 24 underpass and proceed into the station. If continuing the ride west, follow Mount Diablo Boulevard to El Nido Ranch Road.

Morgan Territory Road Panorama (looking West)

Bear right on El Nido Ranch Road and cross through the Highway 24 underpass before continuing west to Saint Stephen's Drive, where the El Nido Ranch Road becomes Altarinda Drive. Follow Altarinda Drive past the Orinda city offices to Orindawoods Drive. Bear left on to Orindawoods Drive and descend past the Orinda School, where Orindawoods Drive first becomes Altarinda *Road* and then becomes Santa Maria Way for several blocks before descending steeply to Orinda Way.

If returning to San Francisco from Orinda's BART Station turn left on Orinda Way and ride a hundred feet or so the entrance of the bicycle and pedestrian bridge to the Orinda Station. Continue along the path to the parking lot and station entrance.

If completing the full ride back to Berkeley, continue on Santa Maria Way one block, past Orinda Way to Camino Pablo. Turn right on Camino Pablo and ride northwest to Wildcat Canyon Road. Turn left and begin climbing steeply and steadily, 2.5 miles along Wildcat Canyon Road to Inspiration Point in Tilden Regional Park. Descend to the Botanical Garden, past South Park Drive, where a last short rise awaits. Climb past the Brazil Room and ride along the flat section of Wildcat Canyon Road to the park exit at Grizzly Peak Boulevard.

Cross to Spruce Street and begin the steady, rapid descent into Berkeley. Watch for buses, cars, and pedestrians, along this busy, winding, downhill section of Spruce Street, particularly after crossing Marin Avenue and approaching the intersection of Spruce Street and Los Angeles Avenue. Turn right on Los Angeles Avenue and quickly descend to the Arlington Circle. Continue counterclockwise around the circle and bear right on Marin Avenue, then ride just over one block to Monterey Avenue.

Bear left on Monterey Avenue and descend gradually to Hopkins Street. Turn right on Hopkins Street and proceed one block to Sacramento Street. Turn left on Sacramento Street and continue to Virginia Street, where the ride ends at the North Berkeley BART Station.

RIDE 16 : MOUNT HAMILTON

ELEVATIONS INDICATED IN FEET

Route and 10x profile for illustrative purposes. Base map USGS 100K. Mar 2024

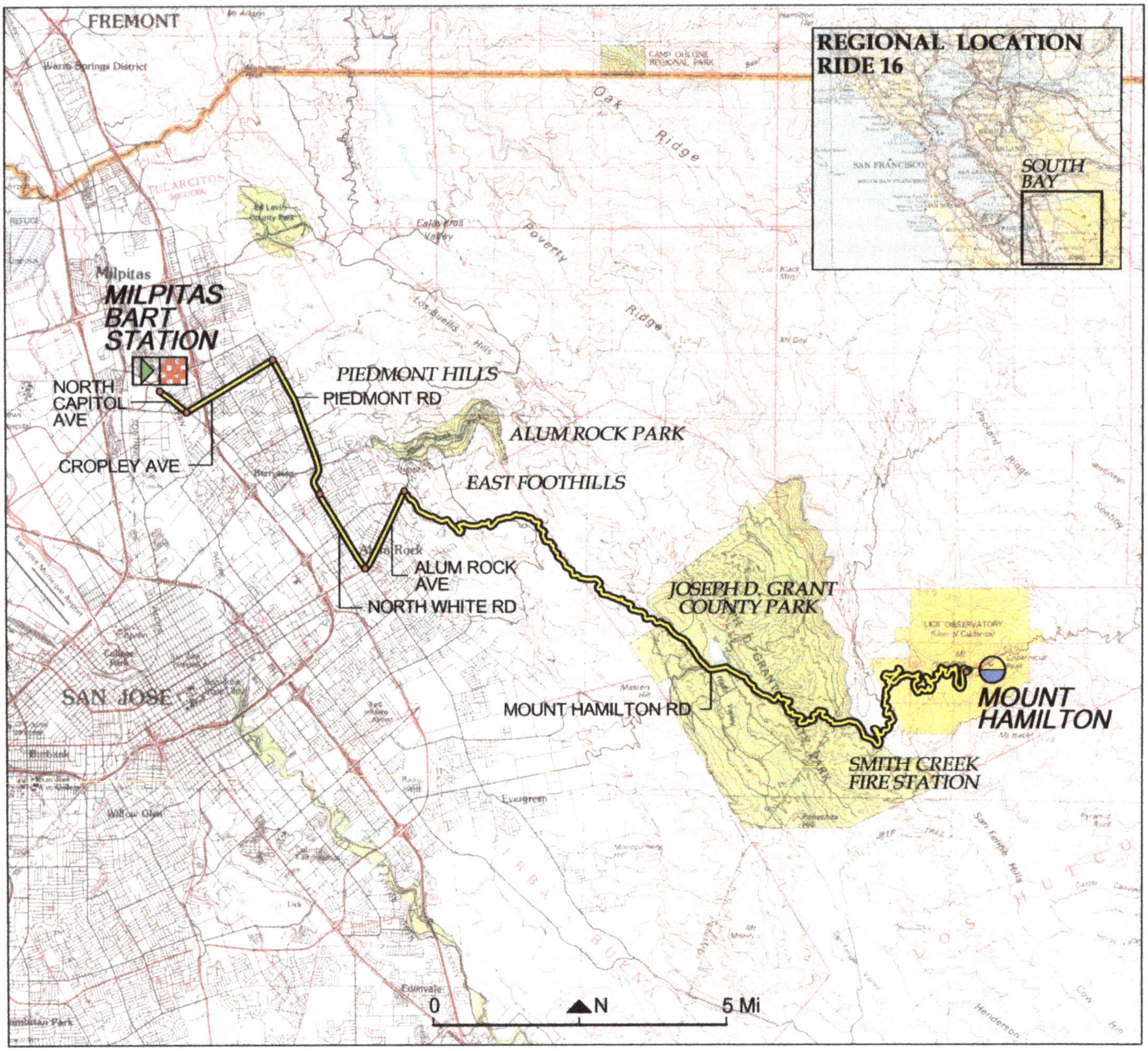

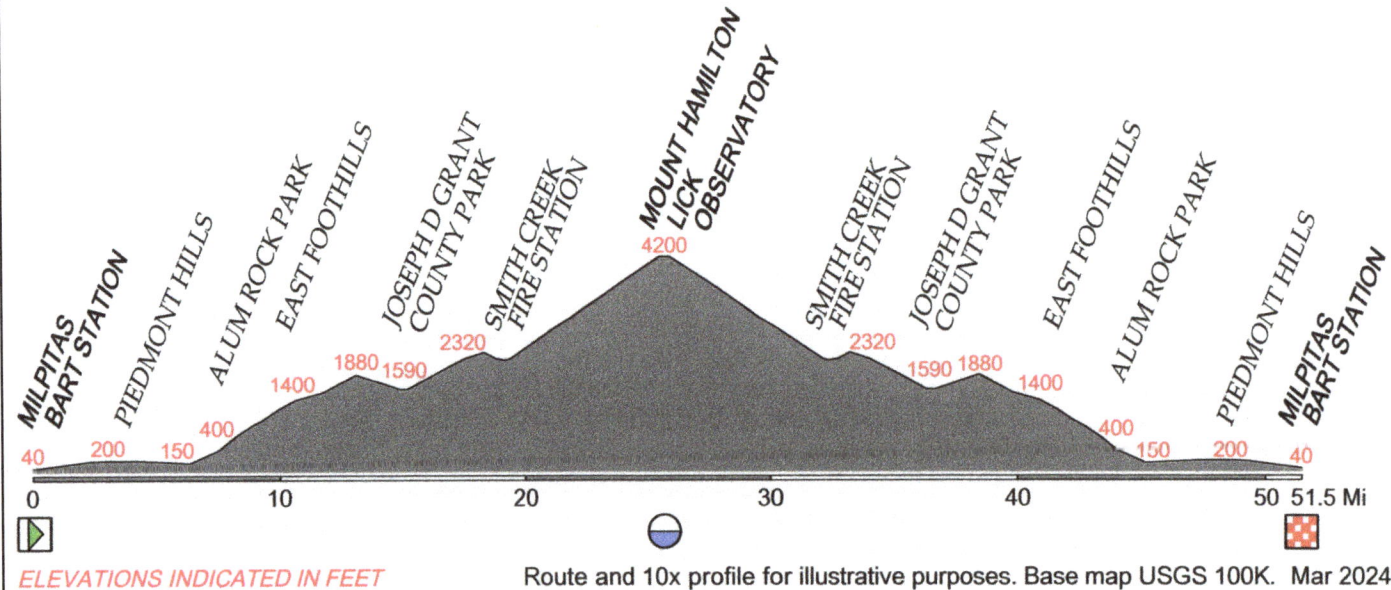

Ride 16: Mount Hamilton

This crowning ride presents a medium distance route through the urban landscapes of Milpitas and San Jose into the hilly parklands of Santa Clara County. The last but certainly not least of the three remarkable Bay Area climbs — Mount Hamilton is the highest peak in the region at an elevation of 4275 feet. The ride to the James Lick Observatory[42] requires sustained, maximum effort on the steep climbing sections and good bike handling skills on the descents. As with Mount Tamalpais and Mount Diablo, the summit views are spectacular during clear weather conditions — the vantage point is above everything else in the San Francisco Bay Area.

Whether ridden as a recreational ride or as training, it typically takes a fit rider three hours or more to complete the climb to Mount Hamilton and return to Milpitas. Some of the more gently-rising sections provide opportunities to glimpse picturesque, pastoral scenery on the climb and the summit reveals long views in every direction from the Observatory's vista point. A medium-distance ride of roughly 51.5 miles, the Mount Hamilton climb is nonetheless tough and memorable due to the 4750 feet of climbing involved and its standing as highest peak in the immediate Bay Area. Some cyclists based in the South Bay make this challenging ride a regular workout — others approach it as an occasional or one-time, high-level achievement.

The route described is simple —it begins and ends at the Milpitas BART Station.[43] Riders proceed generally southeast along the Piedmont Hills to Alum Rock and the East Foothills. Cyclists then begin a hilly eighteen mile climb south on Mount Hamilton Road to the peak. The return is the exact reverse of the climb, ensuring a speedy, but long and technical descent with some climbing as well. Headwinds and traffic can make riding tough work on the flatter final section north to the finish in Milpitas.

Joseph D. Grant Park entrance (looking at Mount Hamilton ten miles up the road)

---

[42] The University of California's astronomical research facility, in operation since 1888, was constructed after a bequest by wealthy California real estate investor James Lick, also a patron of the sciences.
[43] The Milpitas Station is about a one-hour BART ride from San Francisco's Embarcadero Station.

Ride Characteristics

Difficulty: High

Distance: 51.5 miles

Terrain: mixed flat, rolling, and hilly. Several gradual and steady uphill sections within Milpitas and San Jose (Alum Rock). Sustained, steep climbs and descents, along Mount Hamilton Road (Highway 130).

Elevation Range: Approximately 230 feet to 4220 feet above sea level.

Climbing: Approx. 4760 feet

Situation: Urban and urban parkland setting; rural segments of two lane highway.

Road Conditions: Street traffic, moderate to light; pedestrians, moderate to none; roads faces, good to rough, slippery on foggy or overcast wet morning descents throug wooded parklands.

Weather: Sea breezes off the bay and mountain exposure at higher elevations can provide substantial wind factors. Morning conditions can often be cool and cloudy. Summer and Fall afternoon temperatures can be hot.

Notes: Bike shops numbered 52through 55 in Appendix 1 are found in the general vicinity traversed along this route through Milpitas and Santa Clara County. Nevertheless, shops are not always open or nearby — carrying essential tools, a pump, a tire repair kit and 2 tubes is highly recommended. This ride also includes significant segments of rural road where there are *no* services.

Approximate Ride Time: 3 to 4 hours.

Mount Hamilton Road

Detailed Route Directions

Leave the Milpitas BART Station; Begin the ride by crossing the parking lot and East Capitol Avenue. Ride southeast on East Capitol Avenue one block to Trimble Road, where East Capitol Avenue becomes North Capitol Avenue. Continue on North Capitol Avenue to Cropley Avenue. Turn left on Cropley Avenue and ride to Piedmont Road. Turn right on

Piedmont Road and continue southeast. Piedmont Road becomes North White Road in the community of Alum Rock. Follow North White Road to Alum Rock Avenue. Turn left on Alum Rock Avenue and begin climbing to Mount Hamilton Road (Highway 130).

Turn right and follow Mount Hamilton Road approximately eighteen miles to the James Lick Observatory at the summit of Mount Hamilton. The directions are straightforward but the ride itself is anything but simple. Steady climbing is encountered immediately through the east San Jose foothills, followed by a descent into Halls Valley past Joseph D. Grant Park, where the bonafide *ascent* commences — a long, very steep ten-mile climb through numerous tight turns and switchbacks leading to the summit. As you arrive at the crest, turn right on Observatory Peak Road and climb the short rise to the James Lick Observatory parking lot — destination and turnaround point of the ride.

The return ride from the summit to Milpitas follows the climb's directions in their reverse order. Use caution riding down Mount Hamilton Road — the quick descent becomes technical right away. The road near the top is narrow and shady with numerous tight turns and switchbacks, making the descent long and somewhat tense. Good brakes are essential — there are no opportunities for reaching a high speed. Hikers and equestrians often cross the road near the entrance to Joseph D. Grant Park.

Continue northwest on Mount Hamilton Road, climbing through the east San Jose foothills and then descending to Alum Rock Avenue. Turn left on Alum Rock Avenue and ride to North White Road. Turn right on North White Road and ride to Piedmont Road. Continue on Piedmont Road to Cropley Avenue. Turn left on Cropley Avenue and ride to North Capitol Avenue. Turn right and ride northwest on North Capitol Avenue, finishing the ride at the Milpitas BART station.

James Lick Observatory, Mount Hamilton

Index of Selected Places

Alameda County 1
Alamo 101, 109
Alum Rock 115

Berkeley 89, 95, 101, 109
Blackhawk 109
Briones Regional Park 89
Bolinas 63, 71

Canyon 95, 101
Charles L. Tilden Regional Park 89, 95, 101, 109
Clayton 109
Concord 109
Contra Costa County 1, 89, 95, 101, 109
Corte Madera 51, 71, 79

Daly City 1, 25, 31
Devils Slide 32

East Bay 1, 89, 95, 101, 109
Eastport 95, 101
El Cerrito 1
El Granada 31

Fairfax 71
Forest Knolls 71
Fort Point National Historic Site 9

Golden Gate Park 13, 19, 25, 31
Greenbrae 79

Half Moon Bay 31

Inverness 71
Inverness Park 71

James Lick Observatory 115
Joseph D. Grant Park 117

Kentfield 71

Lafayette 1, 95, 101, 109
Lake Merced 19, 25, 31
Lagunitas 71
Larkspur 71, 79
Linda Mar 33
Livermore 109

Marin County 1, 40, 45, 51, 57, 63, 71, 79
Marin Headlands 45
Marin French Cheese Company 79
Marinwood 79
Martinez 95, 109
Mill Valley 51, 71, 79
Milpitas 1, 115
Miramar 35
Montara 31
Moraga 95, 101
Morgan Territory Regional Preserve 109
Moss Beach 31
Mount Diablo 1, 101, 109. 115
Mount Hamilton 1, 115
Mount Tamalpais 57
Muir Beach 63

Nicasio 79
North Berkeley 1, 89, 95, 101, 109
Novato 79

Oakland 95, 101

Ocean Beach 13, 19, 25, 31
Olema 71
Orinda 1, 89, 95, 101, 109

Pacifica 31
Pantoll Station 57, 63, 71

Opposite: Mount Hamilton Road and James Lick Observatory

Pig Farm Hill 97, 110
Pinole Valley 89, 95
Pleasant Hill 1, 95, 111
Point Reyes 1, 63, 71
Point Reyes National Seashore 71

Redwood Regional Park 95, 103
Richmond 89, 95, 109
Robert Sibley Regional Preserve 97, 103
Rockaway Beach 33
Rodeo Lagoon 45
Rock City 105
Rock Springs 57
Ross 71

San Anselmo 71
San Bruno Mountain 25, 31
San Francisco 1, 9, 13, 19, 25, 31, 40. 45,
    51, 57, 63, 71, 79
San Geronimo 71
San Jose 115
San Mateo County 1, 13, 26, 32
San Rafael 79
San Ramon Valley 109
Santa Clara County 1, 115
Sausalito 51, 57, 63, 71, 79
South Bay 1
Stinson Beach 63, 71

Tamalpais Valley Junction 57, 63, 71
Terra Linda 79
The Three Bears 89
Tiburon 51

Walnut Creek 105
White Hill 71
Woodacre 71
Woodville 71

Appendix 1: List of Bike Shops

NOTE: There are well over 150 'bike shops' in the greater San Francisco Bay Area. Some are oriented more towards sales than repairs. This partial list was compiled in 2023/2024 and includes shops that have some proximity to the ride routes described in the guide.

SAN FRANCISCO CO.
1. HuckleBerry Bicycles
1255 Battery St., Ste. 120, San Francisco
415.484-6575
2. Columbus Cyclery Go Bike It
2011 Mason St., San Francisco
415.561-9999
3. Sports Basement Presidio
610 Old Mason St., San Francisco
415.934-2900
4. Roaring Mouse
934 Old Mason St., San Francisco
415.753-6272
5. High Trails Cyclery
1825 Polk St., San Francisco
415.814-3216
6. Trek Bicycle Cow Hollow
3001 Steiner St., San Francisco
415.346-2242
7. Bespoke Cycles
2843 Clay St., San Francisco
415.642-5652
8. San Francyclo [closed]
746 Arguello Blvd., San Francisco
415.831-8031
9. DD Cycles
4049 Balboa St., San Francisco
415.752-7980
10. Spoke Easy SF
1901 Clement St., San Francisco
415.463-5439
11. American Cyclery
510 Frederick St., San Francisco
415.664-4545
12. Avenue Cyclery
756 Stanyan St., San Francisco
415.387-3155
13. Barbary Coast Cyclery
2555 Irving St., San Francisco
415.742-4672
14. Swell Bicycles
4002 Irving St., San Francisco
415.731-3838
15. Elevation Bike Co. [closed]
2648 Judah St., San Francisco
415.702-6132

16. Ocean Cyclery
1935 Ocean Ave., San Francisco
415.239-5004
17. Bike Doctor
2455 27th Ave., San Francisco
415.759-7431

SAN MATEO CO.
18. Gearhead Bicycles
1039 Terra Nova Blvd., Pacifica
650.359-7185
19. Epicenter Cycling
1265 Linda Mar Blvd., Pacifica
650.733-7860
20. Dero Fixit Bike Repair Shops
1223 and 1399 Highway 1, Half Moon Bay
21. Bike Works
520 Kelly Ave., Half Moon Bay
650.726-6700
22. Straight Wheel Cycling
436 Purisima St., Half Moon Bay
650.750-5215

MARIN CO.
23. Above Category
42 Caledonia St., Sausalito
415.339-9250
24. Spearhead Bicycle Excellence
3 Rd. 3, Ste. C, Sausalito
415.342-7618
25. Bikes by Brian
420 Coloma St., Sausalito
415.328-6480
26. Mike's Bikes of Sausalito
1 Gate 6 Rd., Sausalito
415.332-3200
27. Xtracycle
237 Shoreline Highway, Mill Valley
415.326-9717
28. Tam Bikes
357 Miller Ave., Mill Valley
415.389-1900
29. Trek Bicycle Corte Madera
13 San Clemente Dr., Corte Madera

415.927-7433
30. Big 5 Sporting Goods
110 Nellen Ave., Corte Madera
415.924-3221
31. Caesar's Cyclery
29 San Anselmo Ave., San Anselmo
417-721-0171
32. Mike's Bikes of San Rafael
836 4th St., San Rafael
415.454-3747
33. Fritz Bikes
3415 Shoreline Highway, Stinson Beach
415.306-8864
34. Black Mountain Cycles
11101 Highway 1, Point Reyes Station
415.663-8125
34. Bicycle Brüstop
830 Grant Ave., Novato
415.408-3363

ALAMEDA CO.
36. Blue Heron Bicycles
1306 Gilman St., Berkeley
510.524-1937
37. Berkeley Cycle Works
1619 San Pablo Ave., Berkeley
510.525-2453
38. Bikes on Solano
1554 Solano Ave., Albany
510 524-1094
39. Mike's Bikes of Berkeley
1824 University Ave., Berkeley
510.845-2453
40. Lulu's Cyclery
1944 University Ave., Berkeley
510.381-2987
41. Trek Bicycle Berkeley Downtown
2480 Shattuck Ave., Berkeley
510.370-2890
42. Karim Cycles
2800 Telegraph Ave., Berkeley
510.841-2181

CONTRA COSTA CO.
43. El Sobrante Cyclery
5057 El Portal Dr., El Sobrante
510.223-3440
44. The Pedaler Bike Shop
3826 San Pablo Dam Rd., El Sobrante
510.222-3420
45. Big Dave's Bikes
609 Gregory Ln., #120, Pleasant Hill
925.954-1956
46. Clayton Bicycle Center
5411 Clayton Rd., Clayton
925.672-2522
47. Trek Bicycle Alamo
180 Alamo Plaza, Alamo
925.718-8100
48. Hank and Frank Bicycles
3377 Mount Diablo Blvd., Lafayette
925.283-2453
49. Sharp Bicycle
969 Moraga Rd., Lafayette
925.284-9616
50. First Mile Cycle Works
3566 Mount Diablo Blvd., Lafayette
925.385-7072
51. Beyond Aero
85 Orinda Way, Orinda
925.257-7035

SANTA CLARA CO.
52. Dick's Sporting Goods
1200 Great Mall Dr., Milpitas
408.503-0370
53. Saso Bike
14860 East Hills Rd., San Jose
408.258-5574
54. Sun Bike Shop
2646 Alum Rock Ave., San Jose
408.262-4360
55. Fast Bicycle
2274 Alum Rock Ave., San Jose
408.251-9110

About the Author

Jonathan Van Coops was one of those kids to whom a bicycle gave wings. He grew up in the 1960s riding in the San Francisco area's East Bay flatlands. By 1970, he had nailed cleats on to his cycling shoes and began riding his modest French ten-speed road bike gradually further into the hilly Regional Parks and watershed lands east of Berkeley.

A lover of bike racing but not a licensed racer himself, he became a decent climber by necessity and began focusing on longer distance rides in his teens and twenties. Three and four-hour rides covering 60 miles or more became regular weekend workouts. Throughout his thirties and forties he rode constantly and completed the various San Francisco area 'century' rides and an array of west coast long-distance cycling events.

After many miles on that trusty *Peugeot*, he began assembling a varied collection of bikes in the 1980s. At one point, he owned 'primo' steel-frame, *Campagnolo*-equipped *Colnago, Masi* and *Coppi* road racers, a *Schwinn Paramount* track bike, *Santana* tandem, and a pre-WWII *Schwinn* balloon-tire cruiser complete with 'tanks' and horn. These are just the 'notables.' Since 2006, he's ridden another steel-frame road bike, this frame custom-designed and crafted by East Bay master builder, Bernie Mikkelsen.

Repeated hip, shoulder and wrist surgeries during the past forty years have definitely impacted his current cycling adventures. His regular routes have become shorter and flatter but he continues to ride almost daily. Now, at 70, his jaunts on the *'Red Mikk'* are typically in the one to two-hour range, leaving time for his other passions: cartography, writing and preparing healthy, delicious meals fit for any serious cyclist *and* their friends!

The author at Mont Ventoux in France, July 2006

Acknowledgements

Maps, profiles and other graphics by Jonathan Van Coops.

A world of thanks and love to Alina Smiotanko, for her constant supportive energy, patience and participation.

Of course, many thanks to Thomas H. Mikkelsen and Frank Varvaro for their photography, endless review and their enthusiasm for this project. Many of my best cycling adventures took place with these two longtime fellow cyclists 'along for the ride.' Their familiarity with the ride details made their input invaluable.

Guide Information is current as of December 2023. Some information is current as of February 2024. Routes were ridden and driven; some segments were walked. Nevertheless, bike riding conditions constantly change. Updated information or corrections is welcome.

www.ingramcontent.com/pod-product-compliance
Lightning Source LLC
Chambersburg PA
CBHW040226040426
42333CB00054B/3455